Play Therapy with Abused Children

Books of related interest

Training for Good Practice in Child Protection
A Training Manual for Professionals
Edited by Hilary Owen and Jacki Pritchard
ISBN 1 85302 205 5

Child Abuse and Child Abusers
Protection and Prevention
Edited by Lorraine Waterhouse
ISBN 1 85302 133 4

Chain Reaction
Children and Divorce
Ofra Ayalon and Adina Flasher
ISBN 1 85302 136 9

Dramatherapy with Families, Groups and Individuals
Waiting in the Wings
Sue Jennings
ISBN 1 85302 014 1 hb, ISBN 1 85302 144 X pb

Group Work with Children and Adolescents
Edited by Kedar Nath Dwivedi
ISBN 1 85302 157 1

Storymaking in Education and Therapy
Alida Gersie and Nancy King
ISBN 1 85302 519 4 hb, ISBN 1 85302 520 8 pb

Grief in Children
A Handbook for Adults
Atle Dyregrov
ISBN 1 85302 113 X

Symbols of the Soul
Therapy and Guidance Through Fairy Tales
Birgitte Brun, Ernst W Pedersen and Marianne Runberg
Foreword by Murray Cox
ISBN 1 85302 107 5

Play Therapy with Abused Children

Ann Cattanach

Jessica Kingsley Publishers
London and Philadelphia

First published in the United Kingdom in 1992 by
Jessica Kingsley Publishers Ltd
116 Pentonville Road
London N1 9JB

Second impression 1993
First published in paperback 1993

Copyright © Ann Cattanach 1992

British Library Cataloguing in Publication Data
Cattanach, Ann
Playtherapy with Abused Children. – New
ed
I. Title
618.9289165

ISBN 1-85302-193-8 pb
ISBN 1-85302-120-2 hb

Printed and Bound in Great Britain by
Biddles Ltd, Guildford and King's Lynn

For Winsome
who cares about children
and understands the journey

Acknowledgements

I would like to thank all the children who have contributed to the writing of this book.

I appreciate the support my work colleagues have given me as a therapist, coping with the noisy enactments of strange stories and the mess left by 'sticky worms' on walls, doors and ceilings of offices and homes.

Thanks to my family who have always supported me. My children Sarah and Louis for their continued love, Helen for keeping me informed about my grandchildren, and Victoria and James, for the pleasure of sharing some of their childhood. Finally my husband Peter for his patience, love and wizadry with the computer without which this book would never have been finished.

Thanks to Gary Todd for the photographs.

Thanks to Jessica Kingsley for her warmth, support and calmness, to all my friends, especially Sue Jennings, for their comfort.

Thanks to the manufacturers of good Belgian chocolates and French pastries, the best and worst of comfort at the end of a hard day!

I wish to express my appreciation to the following authors and publishers for permission to quote the following extracts:

Bolton F., Morris, L. & MacEachron A. (1989) *Males at Risk. The Other Side of Sexual Abuse.* London: Sage Publications. p81.

Cutler, I. The poem 'Jungle Tips—Piranhas' (1984) from *Large et Puffy.* Todmorden: Arc Publications. p50.

P164, p216, p175–176, p221. Reprinted by permission from the book AWAKENING OSIRIS: THE EGYPTIAN BOOK OF THE DEAD, translated by Normandi Ellis. Published by Phanes Press, PO Box 6114, Grand Rapids, MI 49516, USA, copyright 1988.

Jansson, T. (1987) *Tales from Moomin Valley. London*: Penguin Books. p104–105.

Miller, A. (1988) *The Drama of Being a Child.* London: Virago Press. p143–144

Miller, A. (1990) *Banished Knowledge.* London: Virago Press. p5.

Miller, A. (1983) *For Your Own Good.* London: Virago Press. p97, 98, 100.

National Children's Bureau (1990) *A Policy for Young Children.* London: N.C.B. p1.

Sexing the Cherry a novel by Jeanette Winterson. London: Bloomsbury. p102, p140.

The identifying factors of all therapeutic material have been changed to preserve anonymity

Contents

CHAPTER 1

The Rights of Children and the Abused Child

'Whom are you bringing?' Moomintroll asked.

'It's Ninny,' Too-ticky said. 'Yes, her name's Ninny,'

. . . No one came . . .

'If she's too shy she'd better stay there for a while.'

'She'll be drenched through,' said Moominmamma.

'Perhaps that won't matter much when one's invisible,' . . . 'You all know, don't you, that if people are frightened very often, they sometimes become invisible,' Too-tacky said . . . 'Well, this Ninny was frightened in the wrong way by a lady who had taken care of her without really liking her . . . This lady was ironical all day long every day, and finally the kid started to turn pale and fade around the edges, and less and less was seen of her. Last Friday one couldn't catch sight of her at all. The lady gave her away to me and said she really couldn't take care of relatives she couldn't even see' (Jansson 1987).

In the story of *The Invisible Child* Too-ticky brings Ninny, the invisible child, to the Moomin family:

'And now I've brought her here for you to make her visible again.'

This book is an attempt to make visible the abused child and suggest ways of helping such children feel worthwhile in a world where many children are still seen to be the possessions of their parents or other adults.

It is important for us all to recognise that children are individuals not belongings, not there to fulfil our needs and desires. Children are first and foremost people, but we must also recognise children's developmental needs and their natural dependence on caring adults. Therein lies their vulnerability. When we abuse that dependence, the child's future is damaged.

For those of us who care for children in any capacity it is all too easy to assume a superiority over children, to disregard their feelings, ignore their needs in our decision-making and so reinforce their sense of hopelessness and powerlessness in the face of adult control. Like poor Ninny the child gradually becomes invisible. When that happens we deny the possibilities that lie dormant in the child. In her poetic translation of *Awakening Osiris. The Egyptian Book of the Dead*, Normandi Ellis translates or, as she prefers, meditates on the text about 'Becoming The Child'

> I lie between heaven and earth, between goodness and evil, patience and explosion . . . I know no ending for I have no beginning. I have always been here, a child in the silence of things, ready to wake at any moment. I am possibility (Ellis 1988).

It is the responsibility of adults to develop the possibilities for children and so secure a better future for us all.

The Rights of Children

So what are the rights of children? What do children need to grow and develop and reach their potential?

U.N. Declaration on the Rights of the Child 1959

On November 20 1959 the General Assembly of the United Nations ratified the Declaration of the Rights of the Child. These are:

1. The right to equality, regardless of race, colour, religion, sex or nationality.
2. The right to healthy mental and physical development.
3. The right to a name and a nationality.
4. The right to sufficient food, housing and medical care.
5. The right to special care, if handicapped.
6. The right to love, understanding and care.
7. The right to free education, play and recreation.
8. The right to medical aid in the event of disasters and emergencies.
9. The right to protection from cruelty, neglect and exploitation.
10. The right to protection from persecution and to an upbringing in the spirit of world-wide brotherhood and peace.

This declaration defined the rights of children in their broader sense, as the document was drawn up in response to the plight of children in times of war and natural disaster. Children suffer most at these times, perhaps losing parents, their whole family, and simple, basic care.

U.N. Convention on the Rights of the Child 1989

Thirty years later, in November 1989, the U.N. Convention on the Rights of the Child was adopted. When 20 countries have ratified, the Convention will become international law and binding on those countries which have signed. The Convention states

> the right of every child to a standard of living adequate for the child's physical, mental, spiritual, moral and social development.

The Convention contains more than 30 articles incorporating civil, economic, social and cultural rights. Article 3 *The Welfare Principle* states that

> in all actions concerning children, whether undertaken by public or private social welfare institutions, courts of law, administrative authorities or legislative bodies, the best interests of the child shall be a primary consideration.

Article 19 defines Protection from Abuse. It aims

> to protect the child from all forms of physical or mental violence, injury, or abuse, neglect or negligent treatment, maltreatment or exploitation including sexual abuse while in the care of parent(s), legal guardian(s) or any other person who has the care of the child.

Protective measures include:

> support for the child, and identification, reporting, referral, investigation, treatment, and follow-up of instances of child maltreatment.

Article 34 concerns protecting the child from sexual abuse and sexual exploitation. This is defined as:

(a) the inducement or coercion of a child to engage in any unlawful sexual activity
(b) the exploitative use of children in prostitution or other unlawful sexual practices
(c) the exploitative use of children in pornographic performances and materials.

The purpose of the Convention is to set down minimum rights for children which will be binding on governments. If we examine the UNICEF document 'The State of the World's Children 1991' it is clear that in many countries even the basic needs for food and shelter cannot be met for a variety of reasons from changes in economic structures to changes in climate.

However, the symbolic importance of the document is of value in advocating the rights of children and there is clear recognition of the rights of children who have been abused. In an article on the rights of children Freeman (1987) writes that if we are to make progress we have to recognise the moral integrity of children, we have to treat them as persons entitled to equal concern and respect and entitled to have their autonomy and self-determination recognised. But children, particularly younger children, do need protection.

National Children's Bureau Policy for Young Children

In 1990 the National Children's Bureau published a Policy for Young Children, in particular the under five age group and the principles of this policy are:

- That young children are important in their own right and as a resource for the future.

- That young children are valued and their full development is possible only if they live in an environment which reflects and respects their individual identity, culture and heritage.

- That parents are primarily responsible for nurturing and supporting the development of their children and that this important role should be more highly valued in society

- That central and local government have a duty working in partnership with parents to ensure that services and support are available for families: services that encourage children's cognitive, social, emotional and physical development; and meet parents' need for support for themselves and for day care for their children;

- That services for young children should be provided within a consistent legal framework which allows for flexibility but which ensures; basic protection against pain and abuse; equal opportunities and the absence of discrimination; and the

    development of the child as an individual through good
    quality child care practice (NCB 1990).

This discussion paper suggests that there should be a coherent policy for young children and their families in the fields of health, care and education and emphasises the need for resources to implement policy.

    It is clear that the needs of abused children are not fully met due to lack of resources and while many children are protected from further abuse, the quality of care they receive after abuse can be limited by lack of money or lack of skilled helpers.

The Needs of Children

Children remain dependent on others for a very long time. A baby needs food, warmth and loving care, and the certainty that she will be protected in every situation If these needs are not met the child will adapt, but at enormous cost.

    I am possibility.

    What I hate is ignorance, smallness of imagination, the eye that sees no farther than its own lashes. All things are possible. When we speak in anger, anger will be our truth. When we speak in love and live by love, truth in love will be our comfort. Who you are is limited only by who you think you are (Ellis 1988).

And who you think you are is determined by those early responses to your needs as a baby.

    If we look at the sphere of family life, the writings of Alice Miller, who has received world-wide recognition for her work on the causes and effects of child abuse, powerfully define the needs of children. In the Appendix of her book *The Drama of Being a Child* she states:

1. All children are born to grow, to develop, to live, to love, and
   to articulate their needs and feelings for their self protection.
2. For their development children need the respect and protection
   of adults who take them seriously, love them, and honestly
   help them to become orientated in the world.
3. When these vital needs are frustrated and children are instead
   abused for the sake of adults' needs by being exploited,
   beaten, punished, taken advantage of, manipulated, neglected,
   or deceived without the intervention of any witness, then their
   integrity will be lastingly impaired (Miller 1988).

This statement clearly expresses the needs of children, the responsibilities of adults to meet these needs and the consequences of failure.

So many young children who come for Play Therapy are longing to love and be loved by caring adults and to have friends of their own age, but their early experiences of abuse have left them unable to cope with relationships on any but a superficial level.

Donald was such a child. He had been physically and sexually abused by members of his family and at the age of seven was adopted by kind and loving parents. He longed for love from his parents and friendship from other children but this was very difficult for him to achieve. He was overfriendly, like a young puppy, desperate for affection. He overwhelmed other children with the intensity of his need and demanded constant attention from his new parents, afraid to let them out of his sight. Everybody tried to help him. He was left confused. He said to me,

> I don't know what to do, Ann. Everybody just seems to go blah, blah, blah, blah, telling me what to do. I'm afraid wherever I go because I just don't understand the rules.

He had spent six years of his life defending himself against the violence of his natural father and the contempt of his natural mother and these strategies weren't useful once these threats to his person had gone. But how do you unlearn ways of being, no longer necessary, and when can you trust people enough to even begin to try? His development has been impaired by his early abuse and his future possibilities diminished.

Mia Kellmer Pringle (1974) describes four basic needs for healthy growth in children. These are; the need for love and security, the need for new experiences, the need for praise and recognition and the need for responsibility.

The Need for Love and Security

Kellmer-Pringle describes the need for love and security as probably the most important for healthy development and for the future capacity to give and receive love and affection. Children experience love and security through continuing reliable relationships and the security of familiar places.

The Need for New Experiences

New experiences are essential for the development of the child's intelligence. In early childhood the most vital experiences are through play and language. The child explores the world in this way and through this exploration learns to cope. Going to school opens up a large and more impersonal world.

The Need for Praise and Recognition

The child learns to become a self-reliant and self-accepting adult through modelling himself on the adults who are caring for him. The incentive is provided by the pleasure and praise given to the child's achievements by the adults who love the child.

The Need for Responsibility

Kellmer Pringle suggests that this need is met by allowing the child to gain personal independence, firstly through learning to look after himself in feeding, cleaning and washing. This responsibility is expanded as the child matures until he should be able to accept responsibility from others. Granting independence to the child doesn't mean opting out of participating in and guiding the lives of children. Kellmer Pringle argues that, if these basic needs remain unmet, then development may become distorted and can result in disastrous consequences in later life, both for the abused individual and for society at large.

Donald had six years of unreliable relationships with both of his parents and his brother and sister, never knowing when he was going to be beaten by his father or verbally belittled by his mother. His brother often mothered him but sometimes sexually abused him and his sister tormented him in the same way as his mother. How does he learn to love his new parents in ways that all three find agreable? He doesn't understand the rules, he expects the worst from adults, he has closed himself up because if you don't want, you don't get upset. He has made himself invisible in this torrent of amiable puppy-like devotion. His needs in the past were not met and this has impaired his capacity to love and give and receive affection. And how often do we forget the security of place and routine which make for predictability in a world where so much for the child is new and changing? Through this kind of security the child can develop his or her own sense of identity and personal continuity.

David's mother experienced bouts of mental illness. He was eventually taken into care—and how he missed the streets around his old home. The market, the swimming pool, Macdonald's; these had represented some safety in an uncertain world. He really missed those places! While in care, nobody had taken him back because they were afraid it 'might upset him'. We made a visit together and he was able to walk again through the streets, think of himself as a younger child, remember the good times and the bad and in the future, keep the place alive in his imagination as his 'special' place.

When the child's needs are not met, the child cannot develop a sense of self. Gillian drew a picture about her feelings. She wrote:

> Sometimes I feel like somebody else
> Sometimes I feel like an apple with a worm inside
> Sometimes I feel like an ice cube with a slug inside
> I am a dog
> Sometimes I feel like a pair of old socks
> Sometimes I feel like a tent that people just walk
>   through and leave behind.

The dog in Gillian's foster family had given birth to six puppies and at the time of writing Gillian had seen these puppies depart one by one, given away or sold to good homes and she said she felt like one of the puppies being given away. Other adults taking charge of her life without consultation, nothing belonged to her, people had always used her so even her body felt like a tent that everyone walked through and left behind.

She felt abused physically, sexually and emotionally. Alice Miller (1983) says that all advice pertaining to the rearing of children clothes the needs of the adult rather than fulfils the needs of the child:

> Among the adults' true motives we find:
>
> 1. The unconscious need to pass on to others the humiliation one has undergone oneself.
> 2. The need to find an outlet for repressed affect.
> 3. The need to possess and have at one's disposal a vital object to manipulate.
> 4. Self-defense: ie. the need to idealize one's own childhood and one's parents by dogmatically applying the parents' pedagogical principles to one's own children.
> 5. Fear of freedom.
> 6. Fear of the reappearance of what one has repressed, which one reencounters in one's child and must try to stamp out having killed it in oneself earlier.
> 7. Revenge for the pain one has suffered (Miller 1983).

She points out that children need a large measure of support from the adult to develop their full potential. This support consists of

1. Respect for the child
2. Respect for his rights
3. Tolerance for his feelings
4. Willingness to learn from his behaviour
   a About the nature of the individual child
   b About the child in the parents themselves
   c About the nature of emotional life, which can be observed much more clearly in the child than in the adult because the child can experience his feelings much more intensely and, optimally, more undisguisedly than an adult.

It is clear that many children experience violation of their rights living with adults who cannot meet their needs. Sadly, it is often the children themselves who are blamed or their abuse denied or dismissed by adults and the community at large. The pain of the abused child is too great for us to bear and it is simpler to disbelieve.

An adult says that a five-year-old girl who has disclosed sexual abuse by him is 'A lying little minx'. How sad that the adult is believed and the child disbelieved for no other reason than that she is a child.

The Abused Child is the Invisible Child

To have your rights disregarded is to become invisible, not to count, so the sense of self is eroded. There are two major ways to become invisible: to disappear, or to make the loudest noise. In both situations the child is lost, out of sight in the silence or the screaming.

This is what Amanda said about herself and her brother, both abused by their mother and father. She called herself shit, and sugar is her brother.

Here lies shit and sugar and hag-bag mum,
This is what they did that serves them right

1. Tormented my brother and me
2. Sexually abused us

They made us so afraid that we had to 'kill' them and the only way we could explore our love for each other was through sex.

This is not good if you are a child.

So Sarah 'killed' off her mother by refusing to acknowledge her existence but this left her unable to attach to anybody who wanted to nurture her She was unable to deal with her anger towards her mother so that any adult who took a mothering role was abused and rejected and tormented as she had been as a child by her own mother.

It is not the purpose of this book to examine why adults abuse children. Many extensive studies have been written on why children are abused, examining the reasons from a range of perspectives. Sometimes I see the child disappear in a range of ethological, psychological, socio-logical and political perspectives, lost among the grown ups and their theories about why adults abuse.

These studies are of paramount importance; we must understand the adults' behaviour if we are to protect the children. But often the needs of the children are lost because we find it too painful to acknowledge their hurt. For professional workers, the anxiety is about the safety of children left in the home who are at risk of being abused. Much work is focussed on the assessment of the parents and the risks to the child but sometimes the child gets lost in the process.

Butler-Sloss (1988) stated in the Cleveland Report:

> There is a danger that in looking to the welfare of the children believed to be the victims of sexual abuse the children themselves may be overlooked. The child is a person and not an object of concern.

I recently watched a series of slides, showing children with injuries caused by physical and sexual abuse It was too easy to disregard the individuality of the child in the photograph; perhaps our only way to cope with the shock is to de-personalise the child. However there is a child, really hurt, and we need to acknowledge that. Even by the act of taking the photograph, unless the child gives permission and under-stands their purpose, we are further abusing the child, taking away their rights to privacy and respect. If we have to de-personalise the child to look at the injuries then we deny the rights of that child each time we look at the photograph.

In his book *Child Abuse* Kempe (1978) writes that child abuse involves a hurt child. If we are to help hurt children, initially we have to face and acknowledge the hurts such children suffer. It is difficult for the profes-sional to face some of the cruelties inflicted upon children. If we become too accepting we can become sucked into the abuse ourselves and dismiss its effects on the children. Or we can be overwhelmed by the cruelty and become paralysed and unable to help. In these ways we mirror the feelings of the abused child. There are times when dealing with this form of cruelty can inhibit the way we function in all aspects of our lives. Supervision is essential, supervision of the emotional aspects of the work. We need to be in touch with the abused child and the monster within ourselves.

Definitions of Child Abuse

When helping children who have been abused it is useful to be familiar with the definitions of different forms of abuse, although it is rare that a child's pain can be categorised in simplistic ways. I have never worked with a child whose abuse is not complex and profound.

Any child who has been abused suffers some form of emotional abuse because they are disempowered by the adult involved. Most of the children coming for therapy have been abused in a variety of ways and they often prioritise what for them was the worst terror. For some children it is the blind fear of anticipation, wondering how badly they will be hurt, for others it is the physical pain. Some children fear the humiliation, the cruel taunts of adults. In the case of sexual abuse with young children, it can be the fear of being eaten up or choked or crushed by the physical presence of the adult's body.

Child abuse is usually categorized into physical abuse, physical and emotional neglect, emotional abuse and sexual abuse. Children suffer from an endless variety of abuses, usually at the hands of their parents, frequently without obvious injury and often without complaint. Sadly, some children think that the abuse they receive is a normal part of childhood. Abuse can range from extremes of infant rape and murder, through beating and verbal abuse to the subtle and insidious denial of love.

Physical Abuse

This is defined as any child suffering from non-accidental physical injury. Physical injuries can also be the product of an unsafe environment for the child.

Physical Neglect and Emotional Neglect

Neglect is also maltreatment of the child and this involves failure of the parent to safeguard the health, safety and well-being of the child. In physical terms this includes neglect of feeding, failure to provide appropriate medical care and failure to protect the child from physical and social danger. For example Mrs P left her cigarette burning in the ash tray on a low table where her 18-month-old child played so he was subjected to frequent burns. Mrs P said that getting burnt was the way she taught him not to touch her cigarettes.

In the case of physical neglect, particular attention is drawn to food, hygiene, warmth, clothing, supervision, stimulation, safety precautions and medical care.

Emotional neglect

This includes inadequate nurture, leading to physical, mental or emotional problems; for example, the child's failure to thrive despite an absence of physical causes. Neglect occurs when there is a failure to meet the child's basic needs and implies an omission or indifference to the needs of the child. There could be lack of physical contact, lack of emotional support or recognition of the child as a separate individual. Excluding one child from parental affection, ignoring the child, are causes of emotional neglect.

Emotional Abuse

Emotional abuse involves more active negative attitudes and includes verbal or emotional attacks or threats of attacks. These can include

- ¤ Threats that the child's behaviour could lead to the death or suicide of a parent.
- ¤ Threats or punishment to terrorise the child, such as being locked in a dark cupboard or a confined space.
- ¤ Refusal to recognise the child as a child and refusal to love or give affection, bullying and teasing when a child expresses normal vulnerability, or asks for love.

Sexual Abuse

The most frequently used description is that of Schechter and Roberge (1976)

Sexual abuse is defined as the involvement of dependent, developmentally immature children and adolescents in sexual activities they do not truly comprehend, to which they are unable to give informed consent or that violate the social taboos of family roles (Schechter Roberge 1976).

The definition given by SCOSAC is very clear:

Any child below the age of consent may be deemed to have been sexually abused when a sexually mature person has, by design or by neglect of their usual societal or specific responsibilities in relation to the child, engaged or permitted the engagement of that child in any activity of a sexual nature which is intended to lead to the sexual gratification of the sexually mature person. This definition pertains whether or not this activity involves explicit coercion by any means, whether or not it involves genital or physical contact, whether or not initiated by the child, or whether or not there is discernible harmful outcome in the short term (SCOSA 1984).

The Trauma of Abuse

Children who are subjected to physical, emotional or sexual abuse experience trauma which profoundly damages their lives to such an extent that they need therapeutic help to recover. Children may experience acute stress at the time of the abuse and/or delayed stress.

It is interesting to examine the notion of Post-traumatic Stress Disorder to construct some connections between the stress the children experienced and their later reactions to the trauma of abuse.

Trauma in Post-traumatic Stress Disorder is described as the person having experienced an event that is outside the range of usual human experience and that would be markedly distressing to almost anyone. The traumatic event or events are constantly re-experienced by intrusive recollections or dreams or the feeling that the events are recurring. This creates immense psychological distress. The adult tries to avoid stimuli associated with the trauma and experiences physical symptoms such as difficulty in sleeping or outbursts of anger. The treatment model for adults was described by Donaldson and Gardiner (1985):

1. After a traumatic event, the afflicted person is less bothered in later life if he or she undergoes an ideal psychological processing.

2. This ideal course is interfered with by overly powerful memories persisting in 'active memory storage' when 'processing' does not occur.
3. Therapeutic information breaks the cyclical alternating of denial and numbing and intrusive repetitious thoughts by providing a safe environment in which one can experience the emotional response without automatic denial and numbing of the emotions.
4. Simple conscious recollections, emotional catharsis, or reviews of one's thoughts and beliefs are not enough by themselves but must proceed simultaneously and repeatedly for the best working-through process (Donaldson & Gardiner 1985).

This adult model needs adaptations to specific difficulties experienced by children. Terr (1981) lists some difficulties for children, including fear of death, separation and further trauma, hallucinations of perpetrators. Unlike adults, children do not experience traumatic amnesia, although they do experience psychic numbing if subjected to chronic stress, as is the case for many abused children. Fredrick (1985) described five non-verbal signs of post-traumatic stress among younger children:

1. Sleep disturbances continuing more than several days, wherein actual dreams of the trauma may or may not appear.
2. Separation anxiety or clinging behaviour, such as reluctance to return to school.
3. Phobias about distressing stimuli (e.g., school building, TV scenes, or persons) that remind the victim of the traumatic event.
4. Conduct disturbances, including problems that occur at home or at school that serve as responses to anxiety and frustration.
5. Doubts about the self, including comments about body confusion, self-worth, and desire for withdrawal (Frederick 1985).

My work with young children indicates symptoms of post-traumatic stress are common in abused children. In particular, nightmares where the perpetrator appears or is represented symbolically, occur in the great majority of abuse cases. When nightmares are present, children list them and other sleep disorders as the major difficulty.

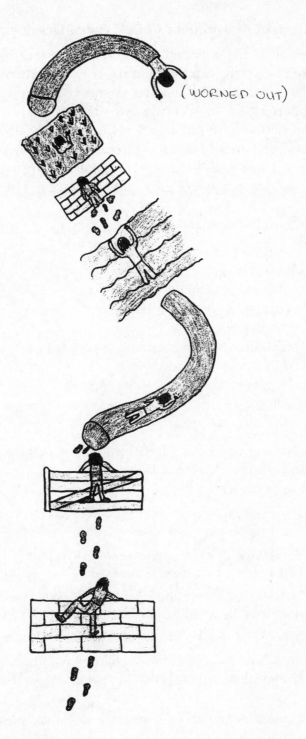

(WORNED OUT)

Figure 1 - Worned out

The Effects of Abuse on the Child's Future Development

Children who are subjected to chronic abuse find the world a very insecure place. Who can the child trust? Everybody must be watched, adults are unpredictable and you can never believe what they say. So such children learn ways of coping to survive.

Colin said when his mother's boyfriends got really angry, he stood by the wall and pretended to be a piece of wallpaper hoping he wouldn't be noticed. Donald rushed around the family, trying to please everyone, distracting and appeasing the adults to prevent violence and family rows.

Judith felt hopeless and bad:

> *A Worm*
> A worm can't run,
> It can only slither
> Just like a great big caterpillar.
> A caterpillar turns
> To butterfly
> But worm
> Stay worm
> Until they
> Die

Martin and Beezley (1977) drew up a list of characteristic behaviour based on a study of 50 abused children.

This list includes:

- ¤ Impaired capacity to enjoy life—abused children often appear sad, preoccupied and listless.

- ¤ Psychiatric or psychosomatic stress symptoms, for example, bed wetting, tantrums, bizarre behaviour, eating problems, etc.

- ¤ Low self-esteem—children who have been abused often think they must be worthless to deserve such treatment.

- ¤ School learning problems, such as lack of concentration.

- ¤ Withdrawal—many abused children withdraw from relationships with other children and become isolated and depressed.

- ¤ Opposition defiance—a generally negative, unco-operative attitude.

- Hypervigilance—typified in the 'frozen watchfulness' expression.

- Compulsivity—abused children sometimes compulsively carry out certain activities or rituals.

- Pseudomature behaviour—a false appearance of independence or being excessively 'good' all the time or offering indiscriminate affection to any adult who takes an interest.

The variety and range of responses as described by Martin and Beezley is the individual child's reaction to the circumstances and relationships of their particular family, but all are ways of coping and survival depends on how well the particular coping style fits the expectations of the parents. The child soon learns that with neglectful parents their needs come first, and she must submit to her parents' wishes.

Many children have very clear memories of the surroundings in which their abuse took place because of their need to be constantly watchful. Peter had fearful memories of his old bedroom and felt very unsafe in his new bedroom. We had to put his mattress on the floor so that 'monsters' couldn't get under the bed and we moved the bed away from the window and near the door so he could make his getaway if he felt afraid.

Many such children become fearful and diffident, accepting whatever happens to them, and totally subsuming their own will to the adults who control them. Jason wrote:

> This pig has no family. He lives in a barn without any friends. They don't like him, they hate him. He wants a family and friends but family more. His family died, cut up into bacon. He is shivering in case he is cut up into bacon. He has lots of hay to keep warm but feels SCARED.

He felt controlled by his family; now he feels controlled by the care system because he can't see a future.

Kempe and Kempe (1978) describe some abused children as having 'demon' symptoms. These children were unable to settle to anything for very long, moving constantly, unable to stand still, constantly trying to attract negative attention, unable to play acceptably with other children. It is suggested that this behaviour may be an imitation of the aggression they received but it certainly doesn't endear the child to her carers. These children seem to come from a background of chaos and uproar and have learned only a negative and action-oriented mode of coping.

Susan was such a young girl. Having been physically abused as a baby, at five years of age she felt she was a very bad child, not worthy of love. To survive in her natural family she had needed to work hard to get anyone to pay attention to her. In her foster family she worked just as hard and wouldn't leave her carer alone for one minute. Attention was her need and whether this was manifested in a reprimand or an affectionate hug was of no consequence. She seemed determined to behave in negative ways, couldn't keep still for a moment; it often seemed that she entered a room and objects broke around her, and the tranquility of the house was lost the moment she appeared. This whirlwind was not easy to live with and it is hard for the carers not to be sucked into her need for negative attention and blame.

The Effects of Sexual Abuse on Children

The effects of sexual abuse on children can be similar to the effects of any other abuse but sexual abuse has particular difficulties, especially sexual abuse within the family.

If children are exposed to unsuitable sexual encounters they are experiencing a type of stimulation for which they are physically and emotionally unprepared. Perhaps one of the greatest difficulties is the reaction to sexual abuse by society at large which then reflects back on the child who perhaps was not aware of the sexual nature of the abuse they were experiencing. The shock and disgust felt by adults at the thought of sexual abuse is perceived by the child as 'my fault'. 'It must be my fault that I was abused because I am so dirty and disgusting.' This dissonance can be hard to dislodge, especially in young children.

The process of disclosing sexual abuse can be a bewildering one for a child, possibly leading to the loss of home and family, perhaps seeing a parent charged with a criminal offence, having to give evidence in court, being asked questions, being medically examined. Much of the initial therapy with a sexually abused child can be preparing for or trying to make sense of the process they are experiencing, often very sensitively handled by professionals but not always so. The court process becomes, sadly, a very bruising experience.

The child feels abandoned, not knowing what adults want them for, often making connections with others by sexual signals and not knowing any other way of making friends. These children's only experience of relationships is that of sexual stimulation instead of parental affection and attention. The sexually abused child feels betrayed, tricked, fearful, vulnerable, ashamed and different from other children. Many young children, abused within the family, feel they are to blame for the abuse and find it difficult to separate themselves from the abuser or find an identity for themselves away from the victim/abuser roles. When they try to make friends with their peers, they have no social strategies other than sexual ones with which to make attachments and this leads to rejection from other children who are puzzled by the behaviour of the abused child, so loneliness increases and the sense of isolation and 'being different' is reinforced.

What Children Say about Their Abuse

Finally, some comments from the children themselves about their abuse and the sense of isolation it brings.

Peter, aged seven:

> Dad hit mum, the police came round. I thought my dad had to go to jail and I wouldn't see him for a long time. My brother came into my bed and the cat came in. My brother said 'Go to sleep' but I couldn't.

Wendy, aged five, sexually abused:

> This is dad. Tell him I do like him a little but . . . but I don't like him really. He hurt me. He wee'd in my bed lots of time. Oh daddy go away. He put me in the cupboard. I was trying to get out and I banged it with a hammer.

Emily, aged five, physically and sexually abused:

> The willy bear doing rude things to the baby. You musn't do that. Don't do that to my granddaughter. The babies grandad did it.

> Poor babes.

Amanda, aged 12, emotionally and sexually abused by family members:

> In a perfect world I don't know if I want to live in a family or to stay at school all the year round. I would like to live in a family not this one (foster family) because I just don't want to live here. I'm not good in families but I don't know why.

> If Ann found the perfect family I would be able to give them nothing I don't suppose.

Louise, aged seven, neglected:

> But she wasn't happy still because she thinks nobody loves her and once she did a very naughty thing—broke her mummy's vase so her mother couldn't look after her so she had to be sent to a different family. In this different family she still felt cross because she still thinks nobody loves her. So she will have to run away again to see if they want her back.

Daisy, aged five, physically and emotionally abused, describing a sexual assault she witnessed:

> I cried and the tears fell down the seat, out of the door, down the road, going on for ever and ever. It was raining tears. Golden tears. They will never stop.

Sharon, aged 11, especially wanted me to write to let children know it is better to tell someone about what is happening because stopping was the best thing for her. However difficult life becomes, nothing is as bad as before. She said to write:

> Speak up. You don't have to take this.

And finally a description from a five-year-old girl physically and sexually abused by her mother and a variety of men, describing very aptly the function of the Play Therapist:

> Once upon a time there was my mum at the park playing on the swings. She bought me a lollipop but it had poison in it and Ann swallowed it instead of me and because Ann understood the poison it went away and she stayed alive and I was better.

CHAPTER 2

Play Therapy as a Healing Process for Abused Children

On the seashore of endless worlds children meet. Tempest roams in the pathless sky, ships are wrecked in the trackless water, death is abroad and children play (Tagore 1913).

The Meaning of Play

Play is the central experience for the child in helping her make sense of the world around her, and her place in that world. Susan Isaacs (1933) states: 'Play is the child's life and the means by which he comes to understand the world he lives in.' As the child grows and develops, she makes meaning about herself and the physical and social world around her, and it is through the medium of play that the child discovers self. D.W. Winnicott (1971) says:

> It is by playing and only in playing that the individual child is able to be creative and to use the whole personality and it is only in being creative that the individual discovers the self (Winnicott 1971).

It is the centrality of the experience of play as the child's mode of creative expression that makes it a dynamic form of therapy for those children who have been abused.

What Is Play?

The importance and seriousness of play is often underestimated, perhaps because the word encompasses activities not defined as 'work' and also perhaps because of its centrality for the child—as adults we undervalue childish things. 'Stop fooling about' we say, 'Don't be so childish' or 'Stop playing about, get on with your work.'

However, play is of vital importance as a way in which we learn to value ourselves. Through playing we can imagine other possibilities and ways of being. These imaginings develop our capacity to be creative. Jung (1931) wrote:

> The creative activity of imagination frees man from his bondage to the 'nothing but' and raises him to the status of one who plays. As Schiller says, man is completely human only when he is at play (Jung 1931).

Play as a Cultural Phenomena

Play as a cultural and historical phenomenon was examined by Huizinga (1955) in his classic work, 'Homo Ludens'. He summed up the formal characteristics of play as a free activity standing outside ordinary life, as being 'not serious' but at the same time absorbing the player intensely and utterly. It is an activity connected with no material interest, and from which no profit is to be gained. It proceeds with its own proper boundaries of time and space according to fixed rules and in an orderly manner. He considered play to be a function of culture from its earliest beginnings, that play is a cultural factor in life and that the spirit of playful competition is, as a social impulse, older than culture itself and pervades all life like a veritable ferment. Ritual grew up in sacred play; poetry was born in play and nourished on play; music and dancing were pure play. Wisdom and philosophy found expression in words and form derived from religious contests. The rules of warfare, the conventions of noble living were built up on play patterns. We have to conclude, therefore, that civilisation is in its earliest phases played. It does not come from play like a babe detaching itself from the womb; it arises in, and as, play and never leaves it (Huizinga 1955).

He suggested that play endured as a new-found creation of the mind retained by the memory. It was transmitted, it became tradition.

Huizinga points out that all play has rules and the rules determined what 'held' in the temporary world circumscribed by play. If the rules of play were broken it robbed play of its 'illusion'. The function of play was as a contest for or a representation of something.

As adults, the form our playing takes is determined by the value our culture places on play and what kind of play is accepted as 'adult'. I am often amused after listening to a passionate discussion of the latest themes in the current soap opera on television to hear those same adults denigrating the play of children, saying it is unimportant and the worse criticism of all 'childish'.

Sue Jennings (1990) points out that 'It is culturally very hard for people to accept that play is something people have to do.' So whether we play soccer, climb mountains, go the the opera, watch television, we must conclude that play has an important function in our culture and in the life and development of the individual in the culture, and that play is an activity essential to our healthy development.

History of the Study of Play

The scientific study of play began in the nineteenth century and perhaps we still suffer from the Victorian attitude which seeks to find a serious purpose for play rather than to emphasise the playfulness of play and the free choices open to those who play, while they are playing.

As a Play Therapist, I experience the attitudes of some other professionals who think that play can't be an important healing mechanism for the child because play isn't serious—not like talking. Talking is a proper activity for adults. Gender issues are part of this attitude; play is something women do with young children, so it isn't intellectually rigorous and therefore is low down in the hierarchy of important therapies. Play is only important as a means to stimulate the child to talk.

Back to the Victorians: Schiller, Spencer and Groos developed ideas about the nature of play and the origins of play.

SCHILLER

Schiller (1875) stated that play was the 'aimless expenditure of exuberant energy'. He considered that young animals and children, because they were protected by parents and therefore not concerned with self preservation had surplus energy which they expended through play. Schiller developed his theory to encompass the idea of the play of the imagination in man. This play had much in common with art. In *Art and Artist* an explanation of aspects of human creativity, Otto Rank (1932) says of Schiller's theories of play:

> Schiller placed the individual between the two worlds of the senses (reality) and the will (moral) to which he ascribes on the one hand the material instinct and on the other the form instinct. The play instinct gives expression and life to both in harmonious union (Rank 1932).

SPENCER

Herbert Spencer, in his *Principles of Psychology* (1873), developed the surplus energy theory by suggesting that play activity driven by surplus energy is directed to those activities which have a prominent part in the animal's life. He also felt that there was an instinctive basis for play and that in play there is a strong tendency to imitate. In man this imitation takes the form of the dramatization of adult activities. These imitations usually take the form of activities the child may be doing seriously at a later stage in their lives. Spencer also emphasised the close relationship between art and play and stated that art is 'but one form of play.' The form in which the play takes place depends on the level of development of the player and Spencer distinguished several divisions of forms of play, namely sensory-motor play, games with rules, and artistic-aesthetic play.

GROOS

The instinct theory of play was developed by Karl Groos in his book *The Play of Man* (1901). Groos defines play as an instinct, inherently part of man's personality and behaviour. He considers that the purpose of childhood is to provide a period for play, that the long period of child-hood in man prepares him for eventual maturity. He also considers that play is related to the development of intelligence.

Groos classifies human play as follows:

A. Experimental play, involving games of general functions such as perception, ideation and emotion. These can be divided into sensory plays, motor plays, intellectual play and emotional play.
B. Sociometric play, involving play of special functions like fighting, chasing, courting, social and family games and imitative play.

J.S.BRUNER

More recently J.S.Bruner (1972) examined the evolutionary context of play in *Nature and Uses of Immaturity*. He states that play appears to serve several important functions. Firstly, it is a way of minimising the conse-quences of one's actions and therefore of learning in a less risky situation and secondly, play provides an excellent opportunity to try combinations of behaviour that would otherwise never be tried. For example, a chim-panzee manipulating a stick in ways which do not necessarily reinforce the use of the stick to probe for objects. Once the chimpanzee has 'learned' to use the stick to probe for food then he soon tries using it to dig, poke other animals and so on.

He also suggests that when animals begin to play, they signal their intent with, for example, a 'galumphing gait' and as play begins the animal can test limits with safety because the group is aware that play has begun.

Child Development Theories and Play

The need to find meaning for play activities has continued in the research on play and this is expressed through interest in play and cognition and the value of play as a means of social interaction.

Playing and Cognition

VYGOTSKY

In *Play and its Role in the Mental Development of Children* Vygotsky (1933) suggested that children's play is a transitional stage in learning to separate the meaning of an object from its presence.

A child plays with a stick, an object, calls it a horse and through using the stick to function as a horse understands the meaning of horse from the presence of the real horse. The child severs the meaning of horse from the real horse and learns to 'think' horse. The stick acts as a pivot and the meaning of 'horse' is established for the child by the play with the stick. The stick and the play are pivots to recall the absent object and the action of the object. Through this the child learns that every object has a meaning. Vygotsky stated that this feature of human perception is called reality perception. I do not see the world in colour and shape only but also as a world with sense and meaning.

PIAGET

Piaget examines play as part of the whole intellectual development of the child and relates play to the process of assimilation and accommodation. Assimilation occurs whenever the individual, as a result of his past experience, is able to recognise and give meaning to new elements encountered in the environment. Accommodation occurs when the individual is changed by the environmental circumstances in which he finds himself. Piaget regarded play as an assimilation of new experience.

He classifies play into three types: practice, symbol and rule. Practice games are used when a new skill is acquired and this begins in the first months of life. Symbolic games are a specifically dramatic form of play and involves the use of make-believe. These games begin when the child is about two years old. The third type of play is social: it involves the rules and regulations imposed by the group and this form of play occurs in the seven to eleven-year-old group.

Representing The Social World In Play

BRETHERTON AND GARVEY

Some interesting work has developed from the ideas of Piaget, examining how children represent their social world in symbolic play. This developmental model examines event representation in symbolic play. That is, the way in which children construct the 'scripts' of their make-believe play and how they represent an experience in symbolic play. Bretherton (1984) states, that in make-believe children use event schemata as new material to create a fictive reality that does not merely simulate but transforms their affective cognitive map of the social world. That by changing various parameters of an event schema, children can create a variety of more- or less- fantastic alternatives to everyday reality (Bretherton 1984).

In this research, the scripts are defined in terms of the roles children take, the actions they perform, the objects they use and how they are all integrated into the play. The level of structure and integration is determined by the developmental level of the child.

Garvey and Brandt observed the way in which children regulate the content and operation of this make-believe play. It is interesting to note their observations concerning the beginning and ending of make-believe play. Children clearly signal that they are about to start playing with statements like 'do you want to play with me' 'it's my turn now', and play ends with a negation of their make-believe roles in a similar way to adults de-roling after a drama enactment or a role play exercise. Children say things like 'I'm not being a monster any more' or 'I'm not dead any more' as a signal that the play is over. Symbolic play is defined as the creation of subjective realities in which the children can experiment with symbolic alternatives to reality and play creatively with these alternatives. Symbolic play also creates the possibility of sharing this make-believe world with others who are also playing. The participants jointly agree to create an alternative reality.

This alternative reality must be marked out as make-believe. Bateson stated that these acts of make-believe are characterized by a logical paradox which he stated as 'These actions in which we now engage do not denote what the actions for which they stand denote'.

Bateson (1971) defined the distinction between play and reality by using the metaphor of the map which is the play and territory which is reality. This defines play as simulated reality. Bretherton felt this was too simplistic. She defines make-believe play as making new maps by transforming old ones.

Play and Dramatic Play

The dramatic nature of play is clearly expressed in theories of Child Drama where play and dramatic play are considered as expressions of creativity developing towards forms of art.

CALDWELL COOK

One of the first innovators in the field of educational drama was Caldwell Cook. In his book *The Play Way* (1917) he states that acting is way to learn, that doing and experience lead to learning and that the natural means of study is play.

PETER SLADE

Peter Slade (1954) defined children's drama as an art form in its own right, in that the child was a natural actor. He makes two distinctions in play, between personal play and projected play. Personal play involves the whole person in movement and characterisation and develops towards acting in the full sense, including activities such as ball games, running, dancing, fighting, and swimming.

Projected play involves less physical activity, but the whole mind is used and dramatic situations are projected onto objects outside the child,. Such activities as art, reading, writing are developed from projected play.

BRIAN WAY

Slade's concepts were developed and adapted by others notably Brian Way in *Development Through Drama (1967)*. He considered that the function of educational drama was the development of the individual through the experience of doing drama. This was a child-centred approach starting from the experience of the child.

GAVIN BOLTON

Gavin Bolton (1979) defines the function of drama in education as being primarily concerned with the change in appraisal—a change in the value given to a situation or concept. He calls this drama for understanding and suggests that, because drama operates subjectively and objectively, the learning is related to those concepts about which value judgements are made. He states that in education we have tended to ignore the affective orientation when teaching concepts. We are training children in the neutral observation of objective facts and so neglecting the personal meanings such concepts may have for children.

DOROTHY HEATHCOTE

Dorothy Heathcote (1980) develops the idea of drama as a social activity and states that the function of drama in education is problem solving: the children are finding a dramatic form to express the solution to their problems. She describes drama experience as an 'as if it were' reality which gives the freedom to experiment without future repercussions and removes the 'chance element' of real life. Through this process children explore their own attitudes, reflect upon living and express their own point of view to produce changes in perception.

RICHARD COURTNEY

Richard Courtney (1985) defined the purpose of drama as a means of relating our inner meanings to social meanings in that we take the perceptions we receive, and re-create them in the mind into imaginings and then express them in dramatic acts. We are able to do this because dramatic action is symbolic. Courtney says that imaginative thought works with possibility internally and that we express this imagining in the external world through dramatic action. He says that the child at play or the student in creative drama is practising with possibility, experimenting with fiction. The dramatic world is not actual it is fictional. It is created out of the possibilities we imagine and then enact. We are indeed the stuff our dreams are made of.

Play as Therapy

Psychoanalysis and Object Relations

FREUD

In *Beyond the Pleasure Principle* (1922) Freud put forward the view that the repetition of symbolic games which children invent for themselves are the ego's attempt to repeat actively a traumatic event which was earlier experienced passively, so the child can gain mastery over the event. He wrote that children repeat in their play everything that has made a great impression on them in actual life, that they thereby abreact the strength of the impression and so to speak make themselves masters of the situation. But, on the other hand, it is clear enough that all their play is influenced by the dominant wish of their time of life, that is, to be grown-up and to be able to do what grown-up people do. It is also observable that the unpleasing character of the experience does not always prevent it being utilised as a game. In the play of children we seem to arrive at the conclusion that the child repeats even the unpleasant experiences because, through her own activity, she gains a far more thorough mastery of the strong impression than was possible through merely passive experience. Every fresh repetition seems to strengthen the mastery for which the child strives.

Child Analysis

Psychoanalytic systems of child analysis developed and used play to interpret the child's unconscious motivation. Anna Freud and Melanie Klein laid the theoretical foundations through their work with neurotic children.

ANNA FREUD

Anna Freud developed a system which uses children's play in a similar way to the use of dreams in adult psychoanalysis. She looked for the unconscious motivation behind imaginative play, drawings and paintings. She also emphasised the importance of the relationship between the therapist and child and did not interpret the latent content of the child's play to the child until the relationship was established.

Anna Freud (1928) wrote that, instead of taking the time and trouble to pursue the child into its domestic environment, we establish at one stroke the whole of its known world in the analyst's room, and let the child move about the room under the analyst's eye, but at first without his interference. In this way we have the opportunity of getting to know the child's various reactions; the strength of its aggressive impulses or its sympathies, as well as its attitude to the various things and persons represented by the toys.

MELANIE KLEIN

Klein stated that Play Therapy furnished direct access to the child's unconscious. The spontaneous play of the child was a substitute for the free association of the adult. The child was offered a selection of small toys to use as he wished during the therapeutic hour. The child's conversation and play with the toys was the equivalent to the adult's free associations. Klein emphasised the immediate use of interpretation to the child without delaying the establishment of rapport with the child.

Klein (1932) wrote that action, which is more primitive than thoughts or words, forms the chief part of the child's behaviour, and that the whole is rather like a kaleidoscope picture, often to all appearances quite meaningless; the content of their games, the way in which they play, the means they use, the motives behind a change of game, are seen to have a method in them and will yield up their meanings if we interpret them as we do dreams.

These systems of analysis use the medium of play to indicate the source of problems rather than a curative factor in itself.

Object Relations: The Transitional Space and the Transitional Object

WINNICOTT

Winnicott described the development of the self in the context of object relations theory. This argues that human beings are, by nature, object seeking and we seek objects for the intrinsic satisfaction of relating. If objects in the child's environment are 'good enough' then the child develops into a person who will seek and find such relations.

It is in and through relationships with other persons, whether bad or good enough, that the human person develops. The child's bodily experiences cannot be separated from and are always shaped and given meaning by and with the child's object relations. Instinctual impulses cannot be distinguished or treated apart from their relational aspects.

At a later stage, the live body with its limits and with an inside and outside is felt by the individual to form the core of the 'imaginative self'.

Winnicott suggests that the child's task in the first three years of life is the development of the close relationship with the mother, then a move to separation and individuation to develop a self possessing its own boundaries and body with an inside/outside. This process of individuation is developed through the use of transitional objects and what he calls the transitional space between the mother and child. Winnicott relates this space to playing and explores the process through which mother and child connect in a therapeutic relationship. He describes the 'potential space' between the child and mother as being the place where meaningful communication happens. It is in this area or space that fantasy and reality meet and are one.

Winnicott describes the first object the child uses, for example, the corner of a blanket, a soft object used for sucking for getting to sleep, as a transitional object, the first 'not-me' possession. This object, though separate from him, is also part of him and the child uses the object in the transition from one state to another where some anxiety is present. For example, going to a new place, or going to sleep.

Winnicott suggests that there is a direct development from the transitional object to playing. He described the development of play as a sequence of relationships with the object world in which the mother figure has special roles. She is there to give back what is handed out, to fit in with the baby's play activities, to be available for the child yet not to intrude and he considered that these play activities were necessary for individuation and for the growth of self. He suggested that there is direct development from transitional phenomena to playing and from playing to shared playing and from this to cultural experiences. He suggested that playing is a unique experience, always a creative experience in a space—time continuum, a basic form of living. Winnicott says that this area of playing is not inner psychic reality. It is outside the individual, but it is not in the external world—the child gathers objects or phenomena from external reality and uses them in the service of some sample derived from inner or personal reality (Winnicott 1974).

Winnicott suggested that through playing in therapy the child can dare to reach back for what he lost or was never given, or for what was too painful to be absorbed.

Non-Directive Play Therapy

Non-directive Therapy emphasises that play is in itself a healing process. It is a way of giving the child an opportunity to 'play out' her feelings and problems and to learn about herself in relation to the therapist, who will behave in such a way that the child is secure.

In this method of therapy, play itself is the therapeutic intervention; play is not used as stimulation for other forms of therapy. The focus of the theory is on the process of play which heals the child.

V.M. AXLINE AND C. MOUSTAKAS

In *Play Therapy* Virginia Axline (1947/69) suggests that the individual has within himself the ability to solve his own problems, and that in play therapy, where conditions for growth are optimal, the child reaches for independence. She writes. In play therapy experiences, the child is given an opportunity to learn about himself in relation to the therapist. The therapist will behave in ways that he intends will convey to the child the security and opportunity to explore not only the room and the toys but himself in this experience and relationship (Axline 1955).

Non-directive therapy accepts the child without judgement or pressure to change. Play is the child's natural medium for expression and in Play Therapy the child can play out her feelings of tension, frustration, insecurity, aggression, fear bewilderment and confusion.

Clark Moustakas in *Children in Play Therapy* (1953/74) describes his work as Child-Centred Play Therapy and is concerned with the kind of relationship needed to make the therapy a growth experience.

This relationship between the child and therapist should be one of respect and acceptance of the child by the therapist. He describes the therapeutic process in four stages. At the beginning of the therapy, the child's emotions are diffused and feelings generally negative.

As the relationship between child and therapist is developed, attitudes of hostility become more specific and anger is often expressed against particular people or experiences. As these negative feelings are expressed and accepted by the therapist, the feelings become less intense.

The third level now begins to emerge. The child is no longer completely negative, and while anger is still there, she no longer feels ambivalence towards people in her life. In the final stage of the process, positive feelings begin to emerge and the child sees herself and her relationships with people in a more balanced way.

The levels of the process occur in the child's play and her emotional behaviour in individually varying sequences and there is much overlapping of levels. The security of the child with the therapist and the safety of the environment are key elements in this method.

Play and Healing

A Model of Play Therapy to Heal the Hurt Child

From an exploration of the roots of play and its importance for the child we can establish a multi-dimensional model of Play Therapy which recognises the centrality of play as the child's way of making sense of her world.

In this model the focus of Play Therapy is towards helping the abused child make sense of her experience of abuse and find ways of functioning which do not re-process the patterns of the abusive relationships.

There are four basic concepts in this new model of Play Therapy which help focus the therapy towards healing the abused child. These concepts are:

¤ First, the centrality of play as the child's way of understanding her world.

¤ Second, that play is a developmental process and in therapy the child moves back and forth along a developmental continuum as a way of discovering individuation and separation.

¤ Third, that play is a symbolic process through which the child can experiment with imaginative choices appropriately distanced from the consequences of those choices in 'real' life.

¤ Fourth, play happens in a therapeutic space, the transitional space between child and therapist, the space to define what is 'me' and 'not me', the place where our creative life starts, where we experience for the first time the psychological significance of art.

The Centrality of Play

Play is a unique experience in our lives; it has a reality of its own as an activity in which human beings explore their identity in relation to others. Play is the place where the child first recognises the separateness of what is 'me' and 'not me' and begins to develop a relationship with the world beyond the self. It is the child's way of making contact with her environment.

Play is a creative act. As Grainger (1990) writes:

> I select an object in the outside world and bestow an identity upon it, so that, despite being mine, it now belongs to itself, and this first and foremost is achieved by learning to play (Grainger 1990).

The role of the therapist is to acknowledge the importance and serious-ness of play and to help the child feel free enough to play. The safety of the place, the toys, objects, the sharing of ideas with the therapist, stimulate the child.

The willingness of the therapist to play as an equal participant, taking the child's ideas seriously, entering into the world of the child while keeping the play safe, is the beginning of a trusting relationship, possibly one of the first such relationships for the abused child.

Play as a Developmental Process

In our model of Play Therapy the developmental paradigm we explore consists of three developmental stages of play, described by Sue Jennings as embodiment play, projective play and role play.

EMBODIMENT PLAY

Sue Jennings (1990) writes:

> From birth to a year old the baby is involved in a variety of explorations of the senses. It can make sounds and rhythms, it can make marks (albeit with food and faeces), and it can imitate. The infant can do all these things before it walks and on walking these sensory explorations gain a larger environment in which they can be developed (Jennings 1990).

The infant explores the world through the senses, then begins to explore objects, materials and toys outside herself and move to the projective stage of play.

PROJECTIVE PLAY

The child begins to discover the external world through the exploration of toys and objects external to herself. Sometimes the play with objects is structured into narrative form, making up stories and dramatic action around the objects, but sometimes it takes the form of embodiment play when the materials are used as a form of sensory experience. So a child might make a monster out of play dough and structure a narrative about the object or take pleasure in playing with the material, smelling, touching, poking, hitting, tasting; enjoying a bodily reaction to the material.

ROLE

As the child develops skill in symbolic interaction with external media, dramatic play develops through family play, the re-structuring of real life events, stories and fairy tales. Courtney writes that when the child at play uses imaginative thought and dramatic action to make choices from the evidence he or she relates the inner world to the environment. Knowledge in other words is not an object but a process, a relationship, a dramatic dynamic (Courtney 1985).

Play is the experience which is the root of artistic expression, and, in particular, the 'let's pretend' of children's play is the beginning of drama.

Symbolic Play

Symbolic play is a way the child can explore experiences of abuse, safely distanced from the reality of her own life-experience. Most abused children in Play Therapy find symbols and metaphors to describe their pain. To find the symbol means detaching from the object it represents and this aesthetic distancing is critical for the safety of the abused child. Appropriately distanced from pain and abusers, the child can explore past relationships in a multi-dimensional way and make some meaning and resolution of her past. Grainger writes:

> In one form or another every human being employs symbols to express things outside the immediate range of their present situation. Whether in the form of verbal metaphor, bodily gesture, or the shape given to a series of actions, symbolism is a way of reaching out from one's association with, or inclusion in, one way of being in order to summon an alternative one, at least in thought and imagination (Grainger 1990).

Symbolic play is part of a developmental process for the child. Play with objects develops from simple action patterns compatible with the objects through a sequence of more complex play until the child can transform objects and make dramatic representations. This developmental sequence takes place over a two year period from twenty-four months of age onwards. Garvey (1977/90) states that these abilities are developed by acting on and interacting with the things and people around him. Their appearance throughout the second year of life indicates that the child is learning to play and beginning to engage in make-believe. But, more, these developments also reflect the beginnings of symbolic representation.

When the child experiences this alternative reality, can experiment with make-believe play, and can assign a variety of functions and roles to objects and people, there is the possibility to transcend and transform experience. For the abused child it is a space to explore the boundaries between self and others, inside and outside, abuse and nurture. Courtney argues that dramatic action creates a fictitonal present out of both past and future. Dramatic play enables students to face life-experiences at a functional and symbolic level. Not only do they 'try out' possible futures and 'act out' problems of the past, but they engage in problem-solving in a deep, personal way through the fictional present.

THE THERAPEUTIC SPACE

When the therapist and child meet to play, two areas of space are defined: the physical place in which they meet and the psychic space developed between the child and therapist. Children set play apart from 'real' life by signalling their intention to play and defining the space in which they play. When the therapist offers a place to play it must be safe enough, with clear physical boundaries and free from disruptions from the outside world.

Gersie (1987) writes that as children we play most easily in the fringes of structured time and in the borderland of common space, such as in an attic, beneath a table, at the bottom of the garden, on some nearby wasteland. There we explore our choices regarding the private and the public, the personal and the collective. In order to experiment we need an area which in and of itself offers few constraints, thereby generating many possibilities. Such a space needs to allow for easy transformation into apparent seclusion, through the creation of actual boundaries, or into approachability by allowing access to others.

The psychic space between child and therapist represents the transitional space described by Winnicott as the potential space between child and mother figure. The sequence of relationships in this space is described by Winnicott. First, baby and object are merged with one another. The baby's view of the object is subjective and the mother is oriented towards making actual what the baby is ready to find. Second, the object is repudiated, re-accepted, and perceived objectively. This complex process is dependent on there being a mother or mother-figure prepared to join in and give back what is handed out.

The next stage is being alone in the presence of someone. The child is now playing on the basis of the assumption that the person who loves them and who is therefore reliable is available and continues to be available when remembered after being forgotten. This person is felt to reflect back what happens in the playing.

The child is now getting ready to allow and to enjoy two kinds of playing. First mother and baby play together, but the mother fits in to the babies' activities, then the mother introduces her own playing and the baby discovers ideas that are not her own. Then the couple are playing together in a relationship.

It is this transitional space that is present in Play Therapy as the child moves backwards and forwards along this developmental continuum to find, perhaps for the first time, a relationship which will enable her to meet and separate from a caring adult, a relationship which is not bound by the pathology of an abuser and victim.

This story by Jamie, aged seven, describes some of the changes:

> Once upon a time there was a dragon. He was very frightening because his fire was green and red, blue and gold, and out of his mouth he spat fire.
>
> This is what the Dragon said:
>
> 'I hate everybody in the world except myself. As for me, I'm the king of everybody and I'll set everybody in prison and just leave them there.'
>
> But when he did that there was nobody to look after him so he had to look after himself. But he found he couldn't cook so he got hungry. He found it was boring to work all the time so he decided to let the people out of prison. But the people were so cross because the Dragon was so horrible. They wouldn't help him. They said he was too horrible, so the dragon had to change and be kind to people.
>
> This was hard and took a long time but in the end he learnt to be kind because he wanted people to help him.

The ongoing challenge for the therapist is consistently to provide a framework in which the child can experience this transitional space and can use this space to heal the hurt of abuse. Children use the space in a special way: they use it to play and the form of the play is dramatic.

It must be remembered that what is universal in this process is not the psychotherapy, but the dramatic play.

Yes - of course -
Play is drama - +
must be dramatic for it to
be useful / memorable - For it
to be regularly used as an
intense experience which acts
                    moment of
as a problem solving + competence
+ clear thought.

CHAPTER 3

Starting Play Therapy:
Settings, Materials, Boundaries

> I like coming here to play with you for two reasons. Firstly you've got great toys, it's fun, and secondly because I get the rest of the day off school (John, aged nine).

Play Therapy to Heal the Hurt Child

In the previous chapter we examined a way of healing hurt children through the use of play. In this model of Play Therapy we emphasise the notion that play is the most important way that children make sense of their world. We emphasise the centrality of play for the child; the fact that children must play.

The form of children's play is essentially dramatic, through the child's capacity as a natural actor. Children use symbolic play to create their own special worlds set in their own time and space aside from 'ordinary' life. They have a clear understanding of the boundaries of play and signal their intention to begin and to end play in ways which keep the boundaries clear enough.

Play is a developmental process which passes through the stages of embodiment play, by the use of a transitional object, to projective play and then to the development of role play. Through this process, the child can discover symbols and metaphors to make some sense of her world and these metaphors are embodied, projected and enacted through the medium of play.

Play is a journey of self discovery for the child (and for those who, as adults, want to keep in touch with the inner child inside us all), a way of making sense of the past, present and future. Play is a creative process and the form of the process is essentially dramatic.

The Therapist

When we commit ourselves as a therapist to undertake Play Therapy with an abused child, we make a contract to share a difficult journey to help the child make sense of her world. This world may have been brutal in the extreme, so that the emotional space between child and therapist may be tested again and again until trust is established. We share this journey of self discovery by playing with the child when requested, by empathic support of the child playing by herself or by offering suggestions to help the child begin to play.

Empathic attention means that the therapist must acknowledge to the child the significance of their play and recognize the symbols and metaphors which have meaning for the child. Thus, the therapist must recognise the seriousness of play for the child and enter into an honest contract to participate in playing as an equal partner. She herself, as well as the child, needs to have the capacity to play and to be free to play and to share the pleasure of the experience.

To join a child in making a journey of self discovery through play is a privilege for the therapist and should be regarded as such. In this model of Play Therapy the play is central to the attempt to heal the hurt child and is not just a stimulation to help the child to talk.

I remember giving a talk about a case study to a group of professional workers in which I described how my client had made sense of his family relationships through play, and one psychologist remarked 'Oh he'd be ready now for talking therapy'. And this was exactly what the boy had repudiated in the first place!

Supervision

The first step to take before starting Play Therapy with an abused child is to find a supervisor for your work. By supervisor, I do not mean a case manager but an experienced person who will help you cope with the stresses of the work and the feelings the work engenders in the therapist. Abused children have experienced distorted relationships of unequal power and in consequence have the expectation that all adults want that kind of power over them. We all have within us the capacity to fulfil that expectation, so always need help through supervision to understand the meaning of the transferences the child is giving to us and what these mean in relation to our life as a whole.

Abused children also have horror stories that they need to make sense of in their play and we need a place to put these stories and in which to lay them to rest. As a therapist, it is a struggle to remain optimistic about human beings and what we do to each other after hearing the children's stories. Perhaps we, like the children, are abused through loss of innocence and we, like the children, feel separate. We lose some joy and happiness which can never be replaced.

Children also produce horrific symbolic images and the power of these images is extremely potent. For example, a young boy of six with whom I am working uses the symbol of being blind, having his eyes torn out, to describe his experience of abuse. He made a story:

> Once upon a time there was a witch that flew on a snake and bit Ann's eyes out and she was blind.

> She cried 'Help, help, I want to see' so the snake threw her eyes back.

These stories are powerful and important for the boy but they are also confronting for me and I need help in dealing with my feelings when I am doing this work.

Clearly, supervision must be entered into with a person who can acknowledge the emotional stress and not deny its power. Play Therapy with abused children elicits very strong feelings for the adults involved concerning the nature of our own childhood, and our feelings of rage about cruelty to children. If we have promised the children to be a loyal companion on their journey, we must acknowledge that it is not an easy journey for the adult and be aware that much of our life experience will be confronted on the way.

Alice Miller writes:

> Not to take one's own suffering seriously, to make light of it even to laugh at it, is considered good manners in our culture. This attitude is even called a virtue, and many people (at one time including myself) are proud of their lack of sensitivity towards their own fate and above all towards their own childhood (Miller 1990).

Assessing the Need for Therapy

The majority of abused children who are referred for Play Therapy will be referred by professionals in the social services and there may be many factors to take into account before accepting a client.

Initially, it is important to recognise that Play Therapy with abused children can only be effective if the child is reasonably safe. Many stressed professional workers will refer children who are in a state of crisis, perhaps still living in a dangerous situation and in no way free to reflect on their circumstances. These children need their defence mechanisms to survive and the most effective way to help is to make an appropriate social work assessment of the whole family and their ability to change. If therapy were attempted in these circumstances the family would probably sabotage the work and it is possible that the child would expect the therapist to rescue her—and that is not the function of therapy.

The decision to ask for Play Therapy for an abused child is usually made at the social workers' case conference when plans for the future of the young child are made. These plans might include attempts at reconciliation with the child's natural family or some members of that family, but at this point for many children rehabilitation into their natural family has already failed.

Many of the children referred are living with foster carers as part of a planned move from a temporary to a permanent home. They have been abused by members of their own family and cannot be kept safe from further abuse within that family. For most young children it is hoped that carers will be found who will adopt them. Sadly, after plans are made, children can often get lost in the care system; families are not found and children feel abandoned and powerless, in a timeless limbo, waiting, endlessly waiting for their voices to be heard. This can be the most invisible time in the children's lives. They are, it is to be hoped, safe from abuse, but are forgotten and lost, their rights disregarded, lost in a system with such limited resources that meeting the needs of children is not a priority once they are safe from further abuse.

Apart from the trauma of abuse, these children suffer the loss of their natural family and, however abusive their life may have been, young children do feel a strong sense of loyalty, guilt and longing for their natural family. Sometimes the children have experienced many moves from carer to carer, all adding to their sense of loss and confusion and a feeling that they must be unlovable. As John said to me:

'I can't live with my mother because she couldn't look after me.'

I said 'What does look after mean?'

John said 'I don't know. I want to be with her. I love her. I must be bad'.

One of the key difficulties of therapy with abused children is that they experience a powerful attachment to the adults who abused them. This is especially true of very young children. Rutter writes that there is the consistent observation that attachment still develops in the face of maltreatment and severe punishment . . . Ethological theory correctly predicts that stress should enhance attachment behaviour (Rutter 1972/91). It would seem that the stress of abuse leads the child to attach more strongly to the adult and rejection from the adult seems to create so much anxiety that it increases attachment behaviour in the child—the powerful intermingling of love and fear.

Timing the Intervention

If intervention is required for an abused child, this must be appropriately timed. If there are complicated court cases and the position of the child is not secured, it is better to wait until clear decisions are made and the child is free to deal with what has happened in safety.

However, if the child is reasonably secure and safe from abuse then therapy can begin and help in coping with the court can be part of the intervention.

Information about the Child

It is important to have as much information as possible about the child and the family before starting therapy, especially about the abuse—how and where it happened and the child's reaction.

Many children have complex family relationships which need to be studied by the therapist. Many details will not be known and will probably be learnt in the play sessions. I spent many weeks trying to understand Wendy's symbolic stories about a Teddy Bear before discovering it was the nickname of her uncle, one of her abusers.

The therapist should receive information about plans for the child and the timing of these plans, especially in situations when the child will not go back to his or her natural family and adoptive parents are to be found. At this time, when the child is reasonably safe and the anxieties of professional workers lessened, the therapist is sometimes marginalised and not given appropriate information about the timing of plans for the child.

Some children begin to show stress about their abuse after adoption, when they start to feel safe. This is often very difficult for the adoptive family if the child begins to act out abusive behaviour and the family needs help to understand the process for the child. This is the time when adoptive placements can fail and the children are once again abandoned by adults or further abused in what is supposed to be a safe family.

Peter went from foster care to an adoptive family when he was three, but this family was using the adoption to cement a fragile marriage. When the marriage continued to be fragile, Peter was abused by the father and emotionally abused and rejected by the rest of the family. He returned to foster care very angry and afraid. Another adoptive family was found but the father rejected Peter at the last minute after he had been prepared for adoption a second time. It was then that I met Peter. His play described a world full of snakes and the best option for the hero of his stories was to find a snake who would be true to the hero for ever and ever. He didn't expect much—not a person, just a snake, but even a snake must be for ever.

Play Therapy must be part of an integrated plan to help the child move forward from the abuse to a more settled future, either back to their natural family or into a new situation, which one would hope would be a permanent family.

Investigations and Therapy

There can be confusion about the function of investigative interviews and Play Therapy as a healing process. I am often asked to play with a young child to determine if he or she has been abused, particularly sexually abused.

This is not the function of Play Therapy. If abuse is suspected, there are procedures to follow and appropriate investigations should be set in motion. It is a betrayal of the child to play and not divulge to them the intention of the play. This further abuses the child.

The proper place for Play Therapy is in the treatment plans for the recovery of the child. It is not the function of the Play Therapist to find out details of the abuse or put pressure on the child to give more information for evidence. However if a child discloses abuse during Play Therapy and this information concerns the protection of the child, it is the duty of the therapist to inform professionals in the social services so that the child is kept safe from further abuse.

As part of the agreed contract between child and therapist I always tell the child that I will have to pass on that kind of information for their safety, but I will tell the child what I am going to do and who I am going to tell before I do it. This makes for an honest relationship between child and therapist which is essential for the development of trust between two human beings. Children's rights must be respected, and my responsibilities must also be respected. If the child knows my responsibilities she can choose what to tell me.

Starting Play Therapy

For Play Therapy to incorporate the concepts described in this book it is necessary to construct an optimum environment for the child.

This must be:

- A safe place for the child, which the child recognises as a play space.
- Play materials which facilitate embodiment, projective and symbolic play.
- A therapist capable of providing an empathic relationship with the child, which means that she is able to be the adult who listens, acknowledges and stays with the feelings of the child. The therapist watches and sometimes plays and she has creative skills especially for dramatic play. The therapist can offer these skills to the child without intruding on the child's own creativity.

Finding a Safe Place for the Child

If the therapist is fortunate enough to have her own Play Room, this can be the safe place for the child.

Ideally, this space should be sound-proofed, should have a sink with hot and cold water, sand trays, water trays, and should have walls and floors able to withstand sand, water, clay, paint and other odd missiles which may emerge from the child's person from time to time.

The difficulty with all spaces is shared use. The space and equipment may not always be available. This institutionalises the space which can then feel unsafe for the child. It is crucial for children that they have access to the same toys and they do get very disturbed if objects or the space changes in any way.

The Small Safe Place

Most therapists visit children in a variety of places and have to create their own safe places in the corner of a room, in a house, children's home, or social services office. So I, like the snail, carry my safe place around with me.

I use a blue mat as a safe place. This is a separate space which is set out as part of the ritual of play. The mat is laid down at the beginning of play and folded to signify the end of play. The mat measures about four feet six inches by five feet. I sit on the mat on the floor with the child. The floor is also a safe place which we both equally share. I remain the adult but we share the space as partners in play.

I judge which children will accept the function of the mat and for older children we sit together without the confines of the mat. We make our own space. However, it is surprising how many older children want to play on the blue mat, probably because I share the space as equal player. Huizinga writes that all play moves and has its being, within a play-ground marked off beforehand either materially or ideally, deliberately or as a matter of course. Just as there is no formal difference between play and ritual, so the 'consecrated spot' cannot be formally distinguished from the play-ground. The arena, the card-table, the magic circle, the temple, the stage, the screen, the tennis court, the court of justice, etc. are all in form and function play-grounds, ie forbidden spots, isolated, hedged round, hallowed, within which special rules obtain. All are temporary worlds within the ordinary world, dedicated to the perfor-mance of an act apart (Huizinga 1955).

The time on the mat becomes special, a place out of real time, the therapeutic stage. When we step on the mat we leave behind the respon-sibilities of 'real' life. The mat itself becomes a potent symbol for healing for the child. One boy of six said:

> I know why the mat is blue. It's like the sky which is beautiful, floating, and the sky is all around, everywhere.

The mat becomes the significant place for the child so it is possible to play in the child's home without contaminating the space in the home with all the feelings of the therapy. When we fold the mat at the end of play then we leave all those feelings behind with the mat and I, the therapist, take responsibility for keeping the mat and the feelings left there, until the next time we meet.

Most children ask to draw on the mat when they leave therapy and the underside of the mat contains all the drawings of children who want to leave their mark.

One young girl who had finished therapy told me that she remembered her time with me and that she especially remembered the mat. When she thought about us playing together, she imagined the mat was flying through the air very fast, and we were sitting together with the toys, playing and flying through the air. She knew we weren't really, but that was how she liked to remember that time. I said her idea reminded me of *The Arabian Nights*, endlessly telling stories making our own magical world, but for her own special reasons. She had healed herself and, as the poet says in the Thirty-eighth tale:

> If you suffer injustice, save yourself
> And leave the house behind to mourn its builder (Trans. Haddawy 1990).

Material for Play

Over the years I have collected a variety of toys, and being a therapist does give you a good excuse to loiter in toy shops and buy toys and objects, indulging the child within. I often spend time playing with a new toy in my study before adding it to my play equipment. Some toys that are attractive in the shop, prove difficult to manage, or too fragile so get discarded at this stage before frustrating the child.

The secret of selecting toys is to find objects which will enable the children to express symbolically some of their fears and feelings about the abuse they have experienced. This often means choosing grotesque objects, slightly 'rude' toys, or the characters from the current TV or film interest. Many of the best toys are suggested by children, sometimes to test the therapist's capacity to cope with the slimiest of objects. They are on the whole not educational toys and some of the most effective objects probably exemplify extreme 'bad taste' for the adult.

I keep my toys in brightly coloured bags, carefully chosen, so the children often say how nice the bags look and this gives me the first opportunity to tell the child they are specially chosen because the child is special and deserves the best. For children who value money and nothing much else at the beginning of therapy I tell them how expensive the bags were. I am starting from the children's value system to begin to make them feel special.

Inside the bright bags are white linen laundry bags, each one filled with a different set of toys. The child can open one bag at a time so that they are in control of their material and don't feel threatened by a confusion of toys spilling out all over the place. Some abused children can be quite frightened of certain toys, so they can control which toys are taken out of the bags and if they don't like a toy can put it in the bag, pull the cord tightly and feel the object is contained. This, for some children, is the first time they can choose for themselves.

I always let the children control the toy bags for themselves and never interfere in the process of selecting toys. I don't share in the opening of the bags because the toys are the children's choice, not mine. Even when they fumble with opening a bag, I give instruction about how to get the toys out rather than physically help them and so take away their autonomy. In the process of selecting toys, I am the watching adult, the children make the choices.

Puppet Bag

The puppet bag contains a variety of puppets to represent those who have power and those without power. Mr Crocodile is always used as the abuser, biting, eating, and fighting his victims. Over the years he has eaten a world of victims but also got bashed over the head as many times. The power of the crocodile lies in his green colour, his slime and phallic shape, his ravenous, open mouth and his sharp teeth.

A model of Rocky, the 'hero' of the boxing films, with boxing gloves on fists that punch is the current favourite for the abusing male. In our play he is rarely a hero, just a violent person thumping his way through life. And he often represents the child hitting back at the world This puppet is used mainly to hit out, rarely in constructing a story. It is not an ideal toy for some children as it is difficult to manipulate but when you can punch those fists, what satisfaction!

There is a cockerel with a huge sharp beak who also bites, consumes and pecks his way through life and he also can be used to enable the child to make very abusive shrieks and screams.

The vulnerable are represented by a grey mouse, a white rabbit and a black cat all battered and bruised through long association with the Crocodile. The softness of the 'fur' and the facial expressions of the puppets make the association of helplessness for children. It is important to have different coloured animals as the grey mouse often attracts white children and the black cat, black children.

Figure 2 - Monsters and Heroes

Figure 3 - Puppets—Abusers and Survivors

I have just added a large, soft dog with legs which the child places round his or her neck. This encloses the child and puppet together facing each other. This puppet is large and very realistic with a soft expression. (He is supposed to be a Rottweiler!). He is very popular with children who find it difficult to communicate directly with the therapist. So far this week, I have twice given the dog instruction about how babies are born and in return he has told me about how his grandfather abused him.

Some puppets seem to represent a mediating role, neither abuser nor victim. A hedgehog seems to be used as a kind of wise but prickly person, giving advice, and there is a small tiger with a soft expression which the children use as a symbol of their own aggression, hiding a softness underneath.

All the puppets are easy to use, the 'abusive' animals have large mouths, easy for the children to manipulate with their hands so other objects can be 'eaten' or bitten. Those big mouths are powerful reminders for children who feel consumed by their abuse:

What a big mouth you've got

All the better to eat you with my dear

Initially, children use the puppets for hitting and fighting, but some children go on to make stories using the characters.

This is a story made up by Ryan aged nine who wants to consume the whole world with his anger, yet also wants to find friends:

There was once a witch and she found a rabbit and turned him into a cockerel. She made the cockerel work for her and then she beat it and the cockerel hit her back until she was dead.

Then the cockerel said,

'How can I be a rabbit again because the witch had the spell that could turn me back into a rabbit and now she's dead.

What shall I do now?' he said.

So he called for Mr Tiger.

'Mr Tiger how can I turn back into a rabbit?'

'Well, well, well, well, you shouldn't have killed the witch. Stop being so cheeky.'

But the cockerel got angry and killed the Tiger.

'What am I going to do now' he said.

*Figure 4 - **Family Puppets***

Then he met Mr Crocodile and told him about the witch and the Tiger.

Mr Crocodile told him to stop fighting so much. But the cockerel wouldn't listen and they had a big fight and the cockerel killed Mr Crocodile.

Just then something happened. Mr Hedgehog came along and instead of fighting, Mr Hedgehog and Cockerel made friends and they gave each other nice strokes and gradually Cockerel began to turn into Mr Rabbit and Rabbit and Hedgehog were the best friends ever.

This is Ryan's aim in life, to make friends, but how to do it, that's the problem.

Family Puppets

I have a bag of small family puppets consisting of parents, grandparents, two children and a baby. A black family and a white family. These are used for family play and enjoyed by some children. Other abused children do not want to play with any representations of people and prefer the animal puppets which gives them greater distance from their own situation and so greater safety in play.

It is interesting to note that although these family dolls are puppets, the majority of children use them as dolls when they begin to make stories. It seems that they prefer to externalise the family at an appropriate distance and can't place their hand inside the puppet and 'own' the family in that way.

Jason used the family dolls to play about the sexual activity he had been forced to watch between his grandparents and he used the boy doll to shout through the bedroom wall to tell them to 'shut-up and stop it or he would get angry.' He was able to say in play what he had never dared to do in reality.

Small Family Dolls

I have a bag of about fifty family dolls, a car they can fit in for journeys and a variety of prams, beds and chairs, a bath, dogs, the odd pig or two and other small creatures collected over the years.

These dolls are very popular for story making and for sorting out relationships, separations, deaths, new beginnings. The dolls can be bent, crushed, buried, and all the complexity of family relationships have been expressed through play with the dolls. I included a car large enough to seat the dolls when it became evident that children wanted families to make journeys. So many abused children move from family to family, both in and out of the care system, that the metaphor of journeys, searching for the lost family, the lost home, the place where I was happy, is part of finding the self.

Fifty family dolls may seem a great many, but most children have lived with several families and require fifty dolls to represent all those moves either symbolically or sometimes just in the form of a sorting-out game as children explain the complexities of their lives.

Emily was five, had been in care for over two years; no family could be found for her, she had lost her brothers and sister also in care and hadn't seen her parents for two years. She rightly felt helpless and often played with the dolls, putting a family into the car. The family were a 'rude' dad, mum, old dad and a little girl and they went on a journey in the car going round and round, never getting anywhere, not going anywhere, just going round in circles. And that is her reality and we stay with the pain.

Figure 5 - Small Family Dolls

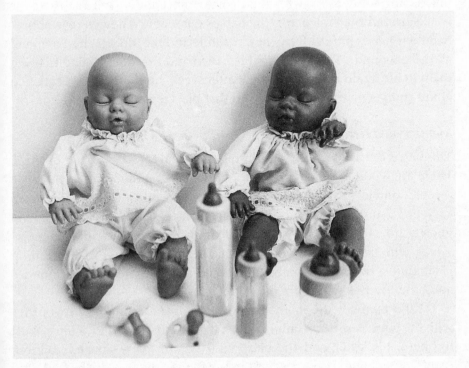

Figure 6 - Baby dolls

Dolls

The bag of dolls contains a black and white doll with plastic heads and soft cloth bodies. Children who have been abused often use these dolls to re-enact their own pain and hit out at the dolls, so soft bodies help that re-enactment. It is important to find dolls which represent the ethnic group of the child. When will the manufacturers of black dolls represent black people and not just dye Caucasian features?

The dolls have a variety of feeding bottles and dummies, mostly actual baby bottles and dummies because sometimes children want to regress to earlier times in their lives and enjoy drinking from the bottles and sucking the dummies themselves. Some children are ambivalent when playing with the dolls, feeding and nurturing them, then suddenly hitting and abusing them, expressing the ambivalence of their own parents towards them.

Children mostly abuse the dolls in the way they were abused, so sexual and physical abuse are re-enacted. Susan, aged five, played with the dolls, always hitting and abusing them. They were bitten by the Crocodile, beaten by her, then nurtured, then beaten again. She phoned the 'doctor'—my role—who had to make the 'babies' well again. As the weeks passed the violence to the babies got worse. They were 'stabbed' had their heads bitten off by the Crocodile and the 'doctor' had to mend all these wounds. Finally the 'babies' died and the 'doctor' had to bring them to life again and again, week after week, until Susan was satisfied at my competence as a 'doctor' and that play ceased.

Monsters and Heroes

This bag is the most used of the representational toys, especially by boys. There are wooden snakes, a variety of witches, spiders, frogs and other creepie crawlers, Shredder the Rat King and other cult villains from current TV and cinema epics. There are monsters whose heads shoot off, ghosts, monsters in chains, mostly recommended by the children themselves. The heroes at the moment of writing are the World Wrestling Champions, the Turtles—interest waning a little there—the Visionaries and other figures which are really dolls for boys.

At the moment the members of the Simpson family are favourites with the boys. A cartoon family with a truly monstrous dad, a mum, Bart the hero, his sister and the baby with whom many abused children identify. Although there are girls in the family, the hero is the boy Bart.

Figure 7 - The Simpsons

Figure 8 - Monsters and Heroes

Each character has a comic 'bubble' in which their phrases and comments are written. This is an excellent therapeutic device, as the children can write their own comments about their abuse or what they feel about family members.

It is interesting that while children want the current TV heroes and villains, their play with these dolls is still the symbolic representation of their own story and not the current TV fable. They adapt the toy for their own needs.

There are very few girl heroes; children's television and films produce too many male heroes but few role models for girls. We are a sexist society. Sometimes the girls use the small family dolls; the princess is very popular. Most girls ignore the male figures and play with representations of animal monsters and animal heroes.

This story is by Roger, aged 11. He comes from a warring family, where you have to take sides and he is really just 'pig in the middle'. He only plays with the Monsters and Heroes and sets them up in battle lines and they fight until there is only one victor. He plays this and nothing else each time he sees me.

> One day a huge army came to attack the half-shell heroes. Michaelangelo grabbed his weapon and charged forward and was soon beaten by a pirate. Michaelangelo sat on the pirate and blew him away.
>
> The other three Turtles grabbed all the weapons and it became a huge duel. Weapons and fists, no blood. The other team were too good and got down the half-shell heroes. They tied them up with live snakes and threw them in the jurk pot with all the horrid creatures. The guards were the two Visionaries trained in every sort of fighting.
>
> One night Michaelangelo tried to escape. The first guard tried to throttle him and was thrown into the Jerk Pit. The second guard had more brain than brawn and bit Michaelangelo in the face then Michaelangelo fell where his brothers lay.

There was another fight between the half-shell heroes and the guards and the heroes won. Everybody is dead except the Turtles.

'We beat them guys, we beat them.'

This seems to me a fair representation of the dynamics of his family. Roger has blurred the boundaries of plot and characters from various TV 'epics' in the way his family blur the roles of parents, brothers, sisters,

*Figure 9 - **Slimy Things***

grandparents to fight and argue metaphorically 'to the death'. We discuss Michaelangelo and his dilemmas as the 'hero' of this continuing epic. Let us hope 'Michaelangelo', like the guard, uses his brains more than his brawn to separate and become his own person. Clearly, not just yet.

Sensory Play

I always bring a variety of play dough and tactile material for modelling, smelling and touching and some jelly-like sticky worms and sticky balls which can be touched, ripped up and generally used in whatever disgusting way the children think fit.

These balls and worms have a jelly-like consistency and can be thrown against the wall or door. The worms wriggle down glass. Children enjoy tearing them and touching them, so I keep a great pile in a plastic bag. Children who want to express anger but are unable to use words find their voice when throwing the objects against the door.

Colour is important and the introduction of fluorescent play dough is a great delight for the children.

I use stage make-up for the children to paint patterns on their faces. I ask the children to imagine their faces are sheets of drawing paper and just to make patterns. I do not encourage children to make up their faces as 'clowns' etc because this requires a particular adult skill and children feel they will be judged. This can reinforce their already strong sense of failure.

Children sometimes ask if I will put the make-up on their faces. I always refuse because they do not have to 'own' the face I have made. It is important for children to feel they are in charge of their own bodies and they can make their own statement about themselves without adult intervention. Children make dramatic faces if given the opportunity to express themselves freely without the constraints of what they 'ought' to look like. Some children who are confused about gender roles after sexual abuse use face-paints to experiment with ways of being, but always symbolically. It's a special way to wonder who you are and what you look like.

The make-up is in fluorescent colours, aqua-paints which can be applied and washed off with water. The colours are powerful, unlike children's face paints which don't give such dramatic results. I always tell the children they are used by professional actors and on television.

The choice in 'slime' is now overwhelming: pink slime, green slime, even purple slime make for the most popular tactile material. Tubs of 'ghostbuster' slime is most popular and has a particular cold, slippery feel. Children use this often to represent the feeling of the world falling on top of you as small creatures are buried under a mound of slime falling out of the sky on the innocent who happen to be standing by.

Children use tactile material to regress to babyhood and play as messily as possible touching, throwing, smearing this material and gaining sensory pleasure from the experience. Children often represent their feelings about their own bodies through this material, slime becomes 'snot', sexual fluids, 'shit'; the sticky jelly balls become sores, lumps and wounds on the skin. They describe the broken bodies, physically or sexually hurt. The pain is brought to the surface and acknowledged, and sometimes the abuse is symbolically played out. Some of the hurt is like the skin of the snake, shed, and in some way it makes the pain bearable.

Sexually abused young children use slime erotically, touching, poking, stroking and becoming sexually aroused. If sex was the only way the children received any sensory stimulation then it is difficult to separate out nurturing experiences. For these children every bodily sensation is sexual and engulfing. The therapist can help broaden the children's range of sensory awareness but recognise that in the beginning there will be sexual responses to certain materials. This decreases as children learn to discriminate

Drawing Material

I have a large collection of felt pens in strong colours and lots of different kinds of drawing paper. The felt pens have a flow like paint which is important for the children. Fluorescent colours and gold and silver are the most popular pens.

Children always say they can't draw and I say that the meaning of drawing on the mat is that it is their drawing and if it belongs to them then it is good.

Play with Toys

These sets of toys are the basis of the material offered to the children. Some children spend many sessions just opening the bags, taking out the toys and putting them back again. Slowly the therapist can encourage the child to begin to play. Some children don't know what to do with toys so need lots of encouragement to begin.

All the children have excellent memories about the toys and woe betide if you lose an object or remove a toy without consultation. Part of the security of play for the child is the therapist's capacity to keep the toys safe so they are always available and never changing. New ones can be added but it is more difficult to remove old ones. The tiniest object is meaningful to some child. This seems particularly so for the children who initially find it difficult to play. For them, the object itself takes on significance until gradually they start to experiment with ideas of 'what would happen if' or 'I could make a story' and symbolic play begins.

CHAPTER 4

The Play Therapy Process for the Abused Child

> My mother groan'd, my father wept,
> Into the dangerous world I leapt,
> Helpless, naked, piping loud,
> Like a fiend hid in a cloud . . .

William Blake, Infant Sorrow

The Play Therapy Process for the Abused child

The play therapy process for the abused child is an exploration through play which helps the child make sense of her experiences in a way which is appropriate to her developmental level. The form and content of the exploration is determined by the child and there are many and varied ways for the child to use play.

Abused children have experienced trauma and containing these experiences can be achieved in different ways. Some children wish to explore their experiences as a way of making sense of their lives; other children want to feel safe now and use therapy as a way of confining the 'monsters' of their past so that they can just get on with their lives, not necessarily re-exploring the past but making the present as secure as possible. Part of the process of exploration is to discover what the child needs to feel safe and contained. The process often seems to me like a journey through a maze with twists and turns, false starts and dead ends until we can reach some final resolution. The Greek myth of Asterion, the Minotaur, half man, half bull living in his house which is a maze seems to me a metaphor for the experience of many abused children who find that home, instead of being a safe place, is like that maze where they are lost and afraid, and in the middle of the maze is the Minotaur, the monster ready to pounce. Nothing like the fantasy of childhood that the adult world wants to believe, as the time of innocence and joy.

Borges in his book of Monsters describes the Minotaur thus:

> The idea of a house built so that people could become lost in it is perhaps more unusual than that of a man with a bull's head but both ideas go well together and the image of the labyrinth fits with the image of the Minotaur. It is equally fitting that in the centre of a monstrous house there be a monstrous inhabitant (Borges 1970).

Stages in the Process

For all children lost in the maze of past abuse there are three stages in the Play Therapy process.

The first stage concerns the establishment of a relationship between the child and the therapist so that trust is engendered and the transitional space between therapist and child is a safe place for exploration. The therapist can become aware of the specific problems presented by the child at this stage. In the second stage child and therapist explore through toys, objects and dramatic play but in a more focussed way, to help integrate and make sense of some of the horror of the past. There is much repetitive play at this stage. The goal of the final stage is to develop self-esteem and an identity not so bound up in the abusive relationships of the past.

The Role of the Therapist

The role of the therapist is to help the child to use the play materials to express herself effectively, to be a player with the child at the child's direction, to be audience and empathic listener when required, to record for the child any stories or explanations about the play, to give it meaning and importance so that the child feels valued.

Sadly, abused children are often offered very little help in making sense of their lives once issues of their protection are resolved, and because they are often initially not adept at expressing themselves with words their potential for learning is overlooked.

I have found that when children play with no sense that they are being judged, when they are accepted, respected and heard, they begin to learn and develop their potential. A critical role for the therapist working with abused children is to contain the play so that children can discharge and make sense of their experiences in safety and at a pace which is safe.

Some children only play briefly about their abuse, then they use the sessions to develop a sense of self esteem and an identity which empowers them.

Preparation for Play

The Contract with The Child

Before any play begins, it is vital to make a contract with the child so that both child and therapist have a clear understanding of their roles and their responsibilities to themselves and each other. However young the child, there needs to be clear understanding for containment and safety. I explain the rules and boundaries and negotiate how we might play together and why we are playing. This includes practical details of time and place as well as the function of the play. I explain the significance of play on the mat as being the establishment of a special place and a special time where we can play together and that because it is special the child can do or say whatever she wants but that there must be some rules for our safety.

These rules are: no fighting, hitting or touching each other, in particular no touching of private parts of the body. I ask the child if they know which parts of the body are private and we discuss this. It is important with the sexually abused child to make very clear boundaries so the child feels safe. I do not feel it is my role to physically nurture abused child so 'no touching' means there can be no misinterpretation of my intentions. Clearly, at times some children do touch and if it is an appropriate touch I accept it but I do not initiate touch as I feel the child must control that choice. Too many adults in the past will have exerted control over the child's body.

I show all the toys to the child so that there is a concrete experience of what is available, then, if we are both in agreement, we can make a contract.

Confidentiality

This is a most important matter to discuss with the child before play begins. I explain that while the play is confidential, if a child discloses abuse or an abuser for the first time then I must inform the adult who has professional responsibility to protect the child. This is always part of the agreement before play starts, and I make sure the child understands.

It often happens in therapy that a child will tell the therapist the name of an abuser or describe more extensive abuse that has happened. I feel very strongly that the therapist has a duty to the child and other children who may be further abused to disclose this information to the appropriate authority, so from the beginning the child knows that any issue of their protection cannot be kept confidential between us. We hope that the children we see in therapy are safe from abuse, but realistically this is not always the case.

I tell the child that if I have to disclose information I will tell them first so that we can be prepared and discuss the likely consequences for the child. Clearly, I discuss this in language which is appropriate for the developmental age of the child but I tell all children, however young, and make sure that they clearly understand. If there is to be trust there must be honesty and the child must be able to choose to play with a clear understanding of what might happen.

I often have professionals ring and ask me to play with a child to find out if they have been abused. This is particularly the case with sexual abuse. I am then asked to do this without the parent knowing. This is very inappropriate, dishonest and indeed abusive, in that it does not acknowledge the child as a person who can choose and undermines family relationships by placing the child in an impossible position. I always refuse, whatever the pressure.

Sometimes children in care or with their natural family show signs of having been abused some time in the past and if there are no issues of child protection, all the carers agree and, most important, the child wants to participate, then I will work with the child. In those circumstances I will discuss with the child the thought that perhaps something abusive happened and we can play to see if we can sort it all out. The child must want to make that journey and be very clear why she is playing.

Starting Play

So we have agreed to make the journey together. We have agreed our roles. I, the therapist, will make the journey as a companion through the maze, not as a rescuer but as a listening adult. The journey belongs to the child; the therapist facilitates and contains the process. The poet Basho made his physical and spiritual journey on his travels and wrote:

> As we turn every corner of the Narrow Road to the Deep North, we sometimes stand up unawares to applaud and we sometimes fall

flat to resist the agonizing pains we feel in the depths of our hearts (Basho 1966).

The beginning is the testing time. Time to test the boundaries, time to test the therapist, time to test the relationship, and time to test the decision to make the journey.

Andrew didn't trust adults. Now aged seven, he had been taken into care as a very young child and lived with loving foster carers who wanted to adopt him, but they were deemed to be too old. He went to a couple for adoption but this failed. Back to the loving foster carers and another couple were found to adopt. The placement failed again so he was finally returned to the foster carers where he will now stay. But how can you believe adults? That's the question—and who had ever asked him what he wanted?

We agreed the contract, then we met in his home for the first play session.

> 'I'm not going to sit on your mat,' he said.
> 'OK' I said. 'No mat, no toys. I'm going home.'
> He gave me a hard, thoughtful stare.
> 'You can stay' he said.
> So I did.

The next week he had another game. He played on the mat, made up his stories, then got off the mat. Very deliberately he placed his foot back on the mat, looked me straight in the eye and said:

> 'You fat old bag.' He smiled and said 'You said I could say what I liked on the mat and my foot is on the mat so it's alright'.
> 'Yes I did', I said.

He tested in this way for several weeks, his language becoming colourful and more explicit. He played touching the mat with as little of his body as possible. I didn't respond, other than to acknowledge the rules. He was very inventive thinking of ways to bend the rules. His insults were imaginative!

Then, after the sixth week, I told him that while I thought he could say what he wanted, and I would survive it, I did find it hurtful. But if he needed to speak that way, then it was fine because he was keeping the rules since he had his foot on the mat when he spoke. I told him that I personally found being called a fat old bag a bit near the bone mainly because I was fat and old, although I wouldn't call myself a bag. I told him that the truth can hurt when repeated as often and as unkindly as he did, but I would still keep coming because that was our agreement. And anyway, I liked him; even though he was rude to me, he was interesting and made up really exciting stories. He gave me a long thoughtful stare. The next week there was no challenge and after play we were sitting together with his foster carers and he said he had something important to say. We listened:

> 'I think children who swear are very immature', he said.
> We agreed wholeheartedly.

He felt empowered; he had made his own decisions but he had kept within the boundaries we had set each other. He had been angry with an adult who had stayed the course and not rejected him as other adults had done in the past. He had shown me his bad side and I still found him loveable. And he had kept the rules.

Susan, aged five, used telling stories on the mat to say all the 'bad' things and use all the 'bad' words when she found it difficult to contain her behaviour at home. She could discharge some of her feelings, but these were still structured in a story so felt contained and she was not overpowered by her sense of self disgust:

> Susan has drawn a tent. I live in it with the dog, cat, parrot, monkeys and gorillas. These gorillas touch each others' private parts, touch and eat poo, smear poo on the walls, and do mushy, pushy, fushy poo, show their boobs, their tits, their willy.
>
> Ann says 'Shove off you old poo bums or I'll smack your bottoms. You do all sorts of things and say poo poo and bum bum.'

Wendy, aged five, had a more fearful reason to test me out. She began each session by picking out the baby dolls and taking a toy knife and cutting the doll's throat. Sometimes the 'baby' died, sometimes she came alive again. I acknowledged her play and asked what happened to the baby. We explored both choice in play, death or recovery. Sometimes my role was to stop the assault, sometimes to accept but never to be afraid. After several weeks that play stopped and Wendy began to explore other stories with other toys.

It was a year later when she told me that her abuser had threatened to cut her throat if she told anyone about the abuse and another nine months before she told me that he had also said he would cut the throat of the person she told. It then became clear that in the early days she had been testing both our capacities to withstand those threats. Much of children's early play seems unclear, confusing, or chaotic but these early explorations need a reassuring response from the therapist so that the child feels contained. The therapist needs to feel comfortable with the 'not knowingness' of these early tentative beginnings. Some children's stories are so terrible that they feel afraid to tell in case the therapist can't cope with the information, so they let out stories gradually out of care for the therapist. Sometimes the horror of the story is too much for the child, who begins to explore ways of dealing with their fear as it is experienced now, rather than recreate the terror of the past.

Alex had been so badly abused by his father, as had other members of his family, that the horror is difficult to comprehend. He was 12 when he came to see me, his father far away and not seen for many years but still his presence was felt. Alex said it was like a ghost enveloping, engulfing and surrounding him. What he wanted was to contain the 'monster', both mythological and factual, who inhabited his dreams and made life fearful to contemplate. We devised ways of coping with the nightmares when his father appeared with a gun and was about to shoot Alex and his brother. We decided that Alex should become Indiana Jones in his dream and, like this character in the film, use his skill with a whip to knock the gun out of his father's hand. Alex was able to incorporate this image into his dream and gradually the nightmares ceased. Alex began to look at me instead of hiding his eyes. He began to laugh. He made a model of the 'monster'.

Then we devised ways of containing monsters in cages from which there was no escape and through games about 'what if the monster tried to break the bars?' and so on, we devised a very strong fortress. Brutal often, we had to make sure that escape was highly unlikely.

As we played games of containing the monster, Alex became more open in his relationships with others and less afraid. He began to talk freely for the first time and gradually began to feel that there was some safety for him and if threatened he could begin to defend himself. We played 'what if the monster escaped' games of what we would do and Alex began to devise strategies.

He realised that at 12 he could kick and scream and shout if he was chased by the 'monster'; he could get away, he had this choice.

This is a beginning and it may also be an end to his exploration of his past—far enough to go when you have experienced intolerable, unbelievable horror and terror. Only Alex can decide how to cope but he has made the decision that he wants to have a life for himself, in spite of the past. He wants to go on.

Sarah. Other children just don't know how to play. They begin by moving around a lot, or testing the safety of the whole room, or looking out of the window at every external noise. But in time, as trust develops, the lure of the toys brings them to play. I am always surprised by the skills of the unconcentrated child to play for an hour when they get the undivided attention of an adult and the stimulation of play objects with no pressure to achieve, even if the play consists of taking out the toys and putting them back in their bags. These are the children who remember every single object and woe betide the therapist who loses anything. All toys are remembered and needed, if only for the reassurance that things can stay the same.

Sarah was such a young girl. Sexually abused, with many secrets and fears, feeling chaotic so trying to control those around her, she couldn't sit for a minute. Gradually, the lure of the toys and the attention of the therapist brought her to focus her energy on play. Some children need these little 'warm up' periods before they settle to play. Others try to control the therapist. Sarah would enter the room and say:

'Tie my shoelaces Ann'

'Tie them yourself' I responded.

Then, satisfied, she would begin to play.

Boundary Testing

Some children do little bits of boundary testing, sliding the toys off the mat and watching to see what happens. I remind them of our rules, and I won't play unless the toys are on the mat. I take this very seriously, entering the world of the child and their rules about signalling play. I talk in their mode:

'I'm not playing' I say very seriously. 'Because you're not playing properly'.

Children accept this because it is part of their rule system, and to play or not to play is the individual's choice. Children often signal 'not playing' by stepping off the mat for a time. I always accept this as 'not playing'. This choice means that children can stay with their feelings without running away because they can still be with me but yet not participating. They can then re-start play but by choosing another set of toys to change the focus for themselves. The image of what is part of the therapeutic journey and what is not is very powerful for some children, who take off the mat those objects or bit of themselves which are not part of that particular story.

The beginning is also the stage when children choose how they will play and which toys are significant for them. Some children systematically play with each set of toys, making specific play with each set of objects. Other children choose particular toys and objects and play with those and nothing else.

Emily, for example, always played with the baby dolls and the small family dolls, adding the crocodile puppet as the 'monster'. For three years she never deviated from those particular objects, which encapsulated all the journeys she wanted to make.

The dolls were battered, nurtured, eaten by the monster, the family dolls went on journeys together, got separated, came together, found new friends, got run over, died in car accidents. All the fears, terrors, fantasies, longings and pleasures of her experience were enacted in play with these particular toys.

Sam, on the other hand, systematically went through each bag of objects, initially desperate that he hadn't missed anything, feeding his greed for play and the touch of the objects, wanting to be recognised as worthy of the attention and love of adults, playing as though his very existence as a person depended on it, as though I would never return and this was his only chance. He was finally able to accept that I would come back and the same objects would be there for him, and his play then became less frantic and more reflective.

Choice of Play Materials

Older children and adolescents who do not use the mat in their therapy still negotiate the materials they want to use and how they might like to play. Some want to draw, others act or write plays and stories use face paint and masks.

David, aged eight, who was physically abused, very street wise and scornful of the idea of play, used face paint to express feelings about himself and his body. He created masks with the colours of the face paints powerfully expressing his sense of outrage about his abuse and the pain in which he now existed. In one session he painted a dotted line around his forehead and wrote 'cut here' to express his hope that some day the pain would cease and he would feel whole again. These are the longings and explorations at the beginning of that journey back into the house of the Minotaur. The journey has many twists and turns and dead ends before we grasp the golden thread and find our way out of the maze. And, in the middle of the Maze, lies the Monster, taking many forms. There are many ways to deal with monsters!

In the Middle Lies the Monster

The middle of the process for the abused child is a difficult, complex, uncomfortable time. Much of the play is about the monster who abused, the terrifying hurt and most of all the enormous loss the child has experienced through the abuse. Loss of autonomy, loss of the ownership of the body, loss of innocence, loss of childhood, maybe loss of the family or part of the family, loss of trust, loss of the capacity to make friends and deal with other children. And often the loss of the monster, because many young children love and miss their abusers. The list goes on and sometimes it seems the road is endless and the pathways blocked as we hack a way through.

Sometimes the way through for the child is to go back to the childhood they might have had and through embodiment play, find ways to nurture the self, using the therapist as the good mother. Children also project that need for nurture onto the play materials, making food from play dough to feed themselves and me. So they too become the good mother, and express through their own senses their physical need for love and nurture.

This play is always present with abused children who are greedy for the love and nurture they missed. The hunger and yearning for love, care and attention can be overwhelming and there is always a corner of the person which can never be satisfied, can never be loved enough.

Some children re-enact both their own lack of nurture, their need for it and the ambivalence they feel about parenting. Children use the baby dolls, dummies, feeding bottles. Dolls are kissed, fed, then hit and abused, loved and rejected in ways the children experienced in their own lives. Other children use the making of food to express their feelings about nurture. They use the play dough to make cakes, pizzas, hamburgers, chips etc. They eat and give this food to me. I have been offered good cake, poisoned cake, earthcake, worm cake, shit cake, 'willy' sausages, 'willy' chips, poisoned pizzas and so on. Often I am given the food and begin pretend eating before I am told it is poison, or shit or whatever.

Delight as I pretend to spit it out, or choke to death, sometimes I am happy to say revived by some magic potion. Love and hate, joy and despair, all the ambivalence, hostility and anger they feel about their own care.

Nurturing and feeding is the pattern often played at the beginning of many sessions to establish the relationship needed to meet the 'Monster' together with the therapist. This nurture time is crucial for abused children who have terrible stories they want to tell but fear that if they tell they might disintegrate or be rejected or be thought disgusting.

Younger children sometimes enact abuse situations immediately they start therapy, as though they must release their stories. They can't hold them any longer. Other children need long periods of nurturing play to feel safe enough to bring up fearful situations.

The most common terrors are nightmares when the abuser appears either as themselves or in the form of a 'Monster'. Other children, as Alex described, feel they are being haunted or engulfed by a ghost. Some children continually remember the abuse or have flashbacks which won't go away.

Daisy, at two years old, had witnessed a traumatic incident when her father had violently assaulted a young girl in the front of a car in which she was a passenger in the back. She began play by painting my right arm red up to the elbow and pretending that my arm was herself. I held conversations with the arm and so did she. Then she selected a doll to represent herself, talked and played with it for several weeks until at last she began an enactment of the trauma she had experienced.

It seemed that before she could go through the recall she had to go back to the beginning and become physically part of an adult then separate from that adult through the transitional object of the doll before she could review her trauma.

Then she made up an enactment using toys, a small car, a police car, an ambulance and small family dolls to represent a baby, a girl and a man. She placed the dolls in the car and the story was always the same:

Baby in the car. Baby crying. Daddy angry. 'Help me, help me.'

This last shouted in a high pitched terrified voice. This story was enacted many times over the period of a year until the fear began to diminish.

Although Daisy was only two years of age when the incident happened and three years of age when she played her story, the intensity of the experience was clear by the power of her play and the terror and horror of the cry for help. The terror of Daisy crying 'help me' was chilling, because the voice was not hers but an imitation of the victim in the front of the car.

At the beginning of the therapy I had no clear details of the assault in the car and it was not clear to me who was crying for help. I asked Daisy many times who was crying. 'Was it the baby?' 'No' said Daisy. 'Who is it then?' She couldn't explain. I gained more details of the incident and eventually I was able to ask 'Is it the lady crying?' 'Yes', said Daisy, relieved that at last I understood.

It is interesting to note that at the time Daisy was involved in the incident in the car, she had no language yet somehow she had heard this terrible searing cry and could mimic the sound. I too will hear it for evermore. It evoked terror.

And the dreams of abused children take many forms; themes of violent abuse and death to the child, some thing, person or enormous monster coming to get you, the child running to escape yet never getting away, being thrown off a balcony to your death; sometimes the abuser himself invades their dream and sometimes some of the dream may be erotic and pleasurable, yet at the same time frightening and beyond understanding for the small child. All images seem to evoke terror and guilt.

Angela, aged five, was troubled by erotic dreams. She dreamed of a large green Monster who performed a variety of sexual acts on her and this dream troubled her greatly because she enjoyed the touching but also felt engulfed and overpowered by the physical sensations. In telling me about the dream and having her feelings accepted as normal Angela felt great relief and her dreams faded and with them the fear that her body was out of her control. However, she still had great difficulty sleeping, afraid that the dream might return and she continued to be afraid at night for many months.

Children's fear of their abusers is not much soothed by verbal reassurances of being safe. The fear seems to lessen after many repeated enactments of the stories and rituals developed in play when the power of the monster is vanquished.

Am I a Monster?

Questions about monsters flow in and out of the play and perhaps for most children the biggest question is 'Am I a monster? I must be a monster for these things to have happened to me. It must be my fault.'

David's monster had six eyes and was very large, but this monster was in fact a child somewhat like David himself so we made up a story where the Monster began to help people by using his strength and size for the good so everybody began to like the Monster because of this.

Throughout all this play the therapist must hear the stories, accept what has happened to the child, say it is not their fault, reassure them that they are not monstrous, accept the good and the bad that the child presents.

Monster Stories

These are some stories, ideas, drawings, enactments made by children trying to make sense of their lives.

Lionel's Stories

These are three stories by Lionel, a boy of eight with learning difficulties. He was physically abused as a baby then later adopted. He found it difficult to be part of a family and was always getting into trouble. Lionel's monster was himself. A monster who nobody could love. He felt he had been turned into a monster by the abuse he had suffered.

This is his first story:

> Once upon a time there was a juggler and when he was little he lived on his own and he was happy. He made a lot of money and he went to France juggling and then he went home. He got his things and went back to France in the circus. But somebody had put a bomb into his juggling set and when he began to juggle he threw the bomb in the air, caught it, it broke and that was the end of him.

The image of the juggler was powerful for Lionel who spent much of his life trying to make sense of family rules and school rules. It must have seemed quite a juggling act to get it right and just when you thought you had got it right—bang—it all blew up in your face and you'd got it wrong again.

Several more stories about the juggler followed and he always got killed by a bomb. Then Lionel began a series of stories about Matilda the

Figure 10 - Lionel's Juggler: Juggling with Knives

*Figure 11 - **This is a mummy monster—she hits you***

witch. So how can you cope with Monster Mothers, especially when the first one hit you so hard?

> Once upon a time there was a witch called Matilda. She turned to Hansel and Gretel for tea. She put them in the pot and ate them up and that was the end of them'.

> Once upon a time there was a witch called Matilda. She had a baby called Baby Matilda. One day Matilda went to the computer and wrote what she was going to do to-day. So she went to the supermarket and bought snakes, spiders, and webs and she made a delicious stew and she ate it. The baby went to the computer and wrote a note and went upstairs. Matilda saw the note and she was angry with the baby and smacked and smacked and smacked her and the baby grew up to be a wicked witch because her mum was so horrible to her.

So monster mothers make monster children. This was his next story:

> Once upon a time there was a boy monster and he was ugly. He frightened everybody sticking his tongue out and he eats people's food and drinks water in the toilet. He swam down the toilet into the sewers into this big machine and this machine cut one of his tails off and he tried to get out of the machine. He couldn't, the machine got nearer and nearer and sucked him up and he died.

> Then one day a magician called Merlin came and said to the monster 'You are not ugly, you have an interesting face and you can make up stories and you can be kind to people'. The monster found this hard. But learnt to be kind and then he had lots of friends and he didn't need to swim down the toilet.

This was the beginning of Lionel finding something worthwhile about himself and lot of stories followed about what makes a person loveable.

Then a final story about his greatest need for unconditional love:

> The juggler was sad because juggling was difficult and he was sad because he didn't have enough money to spend. He only lived with the circus, he had no family. He was a bit happy and sad to live on his own and have no family so one day he went to see a man who bred dogs and he bought a beautiful kind and loving dog who was his companion for many years, The juggler was always kind to the dog and loved him to the end.

Janice was eight. She had been physically and sexually abused, but there were few details of the abuse. In her play she chose three figures from the toys and wove many stories around their relationship. The figures were a witch, a little girl and a bear and this was her story:

> Once upon a time there was a witch who lived with monsters, and she ate little girls. This witch had a pet bear and the little girl had to lick its willy and swallow the food in the willy and this poisoned her and she died.

> The witch cut the little girl up into pieces. Then the willy gave food to everyone but it was poison. The witch also died from eating willy food and she had terrible pains in her stomach and she died.

> The End.

Many children use the images of snakes and witches as symbols of sexual abuse and this does not mean that these children are involved in ritualistic abuse. It is important to discriminate between symbolic play of children expressing what sexual activity might have felt like for a child who does not know the meaning of sexual activity, and the use of rituals by adults as a part of sexual abuse.

Children use those images available to them about bad grown ups and what the abuse felt like. Many children describe abuse as being eaten, consumed, or cut to pieces. Some children have watched very inappropriate videos and some of the images from these horror films and pornographic films occur in children's imagery so that unfortunately it is necessary to have some information about the stories and images used in these films. It is very abusive to expose children to these videos, because they are so emotionally damaging to the child.

However, some children are forced to participate in ritualistic abuse and they do represent these rituals in play. One child used a ritual chant which had been part of the abuse but changed the words and used it as an admonishment to her mother, thus diminishing its power.

Play Therapy is not about getting evidence or information of abuse from the child, so the therapist is free to explore imagery with the child in a way that would be very inappropriate in an investigative interview. The therapy is about healing the wounds and empowering the child.

Marie's Stories

Stories of abused children are sad, about loss of the family, loss of the self, terror, fear, humiliation, horror, trying to understand events beyond comprehension. Family stories express violence, fighting between adults, like Marie's stories. She was nine, in residential care, unable to settle because she was too angry.

She made up stories using the small family dolls to express the relationships she had experienced with her natural family and then in care. Conversation between child and mother:

> 'Can I have some sweets and money?'
> 'No'
> 'Why?'
> 'Because I say so.'
> 'Shut up, shut up you little fat idiot'
> 'I phone the police you bastard. Serves you right'
> 'Fuck off'

And ambivalence. Marie's story about two children:

> 'I'm getting fed up. Let's run away. Get in the car.'
> 'Can I come in the front?'
> 'No. You're too young. Get in the back. Quickly, mum's coming. Quickly.'
> So they run and pack everything into the car. So they all hide under the furniture.
> 'I want to take my pet'
> 'No you can't'
> 'Look out, mum's here'
> They drove away. Then they stopped and got out of the car. The little ones stayed in the car and slept.
> 'Can I sit in the driver's seat?'
> 'Mum won't be happy. This is her car. Let's all sleep in the car. It'll be good. Put the blankets in the car.'
> 'I want to go back to mum. Please.'
> 'No you have to stay with me'
> 'But I want my mum'
> 'No. You've run away'.

The loss of the family is hard to bear. Mum might have hit you, dad might have abused you; you hate them and love them but it's difficult to let them go. Then maybe you are adopted and you are sort of happy, but you don't know the rules of the family and the juggler's baton contains a bomb and you are a monster anyway, because surely only monsters get hurt, so you'll be a monster to spite them all.

*Figure 12 - **This monster is a boy—he kicks people***

As *Jamie* wrote:

> Once upon a time there was a dog called Bonzo and he lived in a family but Bonzo was always naughty. He wee'd on the carpet, ripped the curtains, tried to kill the cat and everybody chased him away.
>
> The family were called Mr and Mrs Brown and the children Rebecca and Peter.
>
> One day they all went for a ride in the car to a museum. The dog ran off and they all began to look for him. They called 'Bonzo! Where are you?'
>
> In the end they found him by the fence. They told him off and he began to howl.
>
> Nobody took any notice and they all went home.

How can the child be heard? The therapist must acknowledge the howl of despair, the sense of powerlessness;

'Nobody took any notice and they all went home'.

So the abused child feels unloved, monstrous and begins to explore what it is like to be an abuser. If this can be experienced in therapy and left behind, the child can go forward to explore parts of themselves which are neither victim nor perpetrator and the survivor emerges. But the power of the abusive relationship is hard to break.

David drew two pictures of himself as monster. He wrote:

I want to be the monster. Sometimes nice, sometimes not.

On his other drawing:

This monster lost his mouth on a bet but speaks through his legs.

The monster was kicking out at everything. This is what happens to many hurt people who lose the power to express their hurt. However, for David we managed finally to change. He began using his legs for kicking a football which he did with skill and with this new skill he found his voice again. And his voice, for most of the time, was neither abused nor abusing.

A really smelly story was created by *Jason* a twelve-year-old boy with learning difficulties who had lived with his mother in fairly squalid circumstances:

Once upon a time there was a monster called Slime. And every day he had to eat slime. If he didn't get enough, he died.

One day he is eating loads of slime until he got stomach ache and then he was sick. And slime splattered everywhere in his bedroom. On the window, all over the sheets, on the walls, and the telly. His mate Slimer came. Phew what a stink. Then Slimer was sick again until the whole room was covered with sick then Slime and Slimer cleaned it up with a shovel and a bucket.

These images often appear with children who have been neglected. *David* began play therapy by using face paint to paint his face green then he would wipe the green face paint on the inside of his mouth and finally spew out green saliva onto a paper towel. He did this for many sessions then began to draw his six eyed monster who was unable to make friends and frightened everybody. Children play with these symbolic monsters, firstly inventing the creature, then being afraid of it, then controlling it. Once the monster is under control the child wants to be it and control others. There is much changing of roles, being the monster, then attacking it, then being the monster again until there is some symbolic under-standing of the processes of the monster and the processes of the monster's victims.

Losing the Monster

Stuart's Story

The stories go on for as long as it takes. Then one day the child says that they don't want to play that any more. For a year, Stuart acted many stories about a family who went from the good world to the bad world and back to the good world again. The family moved from the good world to the bad world when a snake bit the dad in the arm. The way out of the bad world was when the power of the snake diminished. Stuart devised this story as a way of understanding his abuse, which happened when his parents were under the influence of heroin. After about a year he had written and acted his story for many sessions. Then he said that he didn't want to play it any more, that he had finished with it. He had resolved as best he could through his symbolic stories what had gone on in his life which, before the stories, seemed to be meaningless.

Stuart then began to play about himself in the present, what kind of person he was, was he loveable, would he find somebody who would give him unconditional love? He began a series of stories around these themes.

The Final Stage of Play

This is the final stage of play, to explore the identity of the child, not bound by the stereotype of abused or abusing, but an identity which includes other ways of being. Sometimes, at this stage of the work with older children from about six years of age, we play more structured cognitive games to sort out who we are and what we like. So *Lionel* wrote:

> I am Lionel
> I am nice
> I am silly
> I am adopted
> I am a brother
> I am small
> I am good sometimes

> I am a kisser
> I am funny sometimes
> I am a clown sometimes
> I am the son of a mother who hit me
> I am the son of parents who didn't look after me
> I am a cook
> What are you like?

Amanda, aged 12, wrote:

> I am Amanda
> I am small
> I am fat
> I am the daughter of an abusing mother
> I am the daughter of a mother who was abused by her mother
> I am a pain sometimes
> I am an outsider trying to be an insider
> I am sometimes funny
> I am sometimes very bad tempered
> I am ugly
> I am quite good at gymnastics
> I am good at writing stories
> I am creative
> I am a sister
> Sometimes I feel happy
> Sometimes I get very over excited
> Sometimes I used to feel sexy
> Sometimes I enjoy talking sexy
> I am a good friend
> What are you like?

Together we can examine some of the child's values and help her see the distortions in her thinking about herself and the abuse. This is a stage of the therapy where the therapist might encourage the child to re-explore embodiment play to gain new insight into their physical self, regarding their own body and their own sense experiences anew, knowing by now that their play will be respected by the therapist. Simple pleasures such as blowing bubbles, playing with paint, using clay, making a mess eating jelly can offer some small compensation for a lost childhood.

Figure 13 - This is how I draw myself. I have a head and a vagina. My brother has a head and a penis. I shout 'No, no!'

Many abused children are not aware of what they look like, having dampened their sense of their own physical presence to avoid some of the pain of their abuse. One child aged six who had been sexually abused only ever drew her head and vagina and the head and penis of her abuser. As she leaves the abuse behind she can rediscover her body, take pride in it knowing that now it belongs to herself.

Becoming Visible

The invisible child becomes visible. She has a body, she knows how tall she is, what kind of clothes she likes to wear. She can begin to share these ideas and be heard. These may be very simple pleasures, often forgotten by the adult concerned with adult preoccupations about abuse, but for the child this pride in self is an affirmation of her rights as a person. Children at this stage begin to make up stories which contain ideas about their future. Many abused children will not return to their natural parents and are placed for adoption. Their concerns are about parents, will they be loved, are they loveable, how must they behave?

Stuart who had resolved many issues about his own sexual abuse through play became concerned about living with another family and began a series of play enactments about a boy who was getting into all kinds of trouble with the police, who then phoned his mother, (my role). The function of the mother in these stories was to come and defend the boy and get him out of scrapes and take him back home. Stuart was in the process of finding a family who might adopt him, so his concerns were around how loveable he was and if he could hope for unconditional love from his new family. In fact, he has found such a family. After being rejected by one prospective family, the foster family who had cared and loved him unconditionally for two years chose to adopt him. This was the perfect answer for him.

In Stuart's stories about his abuse he had defined the experience of the abuse as the family going from the good world into the bad world. When he knew he was to be adopted and we finished our therapy, he restructured his story of the good and bad world for the last time. He felt he was powerful and soaring like a bird and as a bird he told the story:

A bird told the story.

Remember the time the good world turned into the Bad World. The snake at the entrance to the Bad World transformed the mum and bad dad from people into snakes. Well this time the snake transformed them and they stayed in the Bad World for ever and ever. Bad Dad changed into a snake and Mum followed him and turned into a snake.

Then the bird went to the Bad World and said goodbye to the two snakes.

'You're on your own now. Good luck and goodbye'.

Stuart still remained generous to the two people who had abused and terrorised him so badly as a young child. While acknowledging their violence and abuse and the lifestyle they had chosen, he still wished them well.

Many children who have been abused have never had much chance to say goodbye to anyone without taking on a burden of guilt or feeling that the separation was their fault. Sometimes abused children are removed from their natural family amid dramatic scenes, or with police presence and they may go from foster placement to foster placement without making much sense of their experiences.

It is very important that therapeutic endings should be positive and empowering for the child; in many cases it may, perhaps, be the first time they have made a good separation. *Susan* had never separated from anybody with a good ending. She had been taken from her mother with little explanation; in fact, she thought she had killed her brother and that that was the reason she was placed in a children's home. Her time in the children's home also proved to be abusive and she was placed with foster carers, who have loved and cared for her and fought for her rights, but her first four years were a catalogue of abuse.

The time came for us to end the therapy and say goodbye. I spent many sessions preparing her for the parting, and this was reinforced by her foster family. Susan associated parting with death and the belief that she, Susan, was responsible for that death.

I had to explain that when I left for the last time it didn't mean that I had died, that I would be playing with other children who needed help and she could think of me doing that when I didn't see her any more. I told her that we had finished playing together because she was settled with her family and would stay there and she didn't need my help any more. We had a happy last meeting giving and accepting presents and cards and she now proudly tells her friends all the reasons why she doesn't see me and what I am doing instead of seeing her.

David was eight when we said goodbye. He was no longer the green monster who spewed green slime but a boy who kicked a football exceptionally well instead of kicking people. He had missed so many nurturing experiences as a baby that he decided our last meeting would be a celebration of feeding greed. I agreed, being no slouch in the greed game myself and I brought a large bag of wonderful Woolworth jelly sweets, wriggly cocacola worms, jelly insects, jelly babies; all manner of sweets and we sucked them and slurped them and played with them as small children and laughed and smiled and were messy together. It was fun and we could express our sadness at leaving each other but end with a smile and affection.

So ending brings some sense of resolution, leaving behind some of the ghosts, finding ways to cope with the monsters inside ourselves and the monsters who abused. There are many ways to deal with these monsters. Laughter is one. As Ivor Cutler writes in *Jungle Tips—Piranhas*:

> If you are wading across the Amazon, and a school of piranhas starts to take an interest, hum like mad whilst spilling a bottle of tomato ketchup across the river. They will imagine that you are another bleeding humming-bird, and will shun you as they cannot abide feathers stuck to their teeth (Cutler 1984).

The way through the labyrinth, to meet the Monster, then leave him behind and find a way out leads to other journeys for the child in which the therapist will not be a companion along the way. For the abused child, I hope for recognition and enough resolution to go on.

> Even night and day struggle, make peace between themselves. We call that beautiful sunset and dawn. In the spirits of men we call it a state of grace. Unless the earth enveloped the seed and the seed struggled against the darkness, there would be no corn. The moment we are born we begin to die. In each death we are born again. We take in the air and the air escapes us. Call it the breath of life. I no longer call it disaster. It is the empty heart waiting to be filled (Trans. Ellis 1988).

CHAPTER 5

Play Therapy With Physically Abused Children

> Did my childhood happen? I must believe it did, but I don't have any proof. My mother says it did, but she is a fantasist, a liar and a murderer, though none of that would stop me loving her' (Winterson 1989).

Small children who have suffered the trauma of severe physical abuse are usually protected from further abuse by being removed from their family and taken into care. The pain of the abuse—the scalding water, the cigarette burns, being thrown across the room, burnt with the poker, being beaten once too often—at least that is over now. But they may also lose their parents, possibly daily contact with brothers and sisters and the place in which they lived. To be safe, the child can lose everything.

The loss of the parents can bring relief from fear but a strong sense of emptiness. The powerful bonding created through fear: the terror, confusion, tears, begging for forgiveness is all gone in a flash. No comfort of familiar surroundings, no sharing with brothers and sisters. What is going to happen? It's my fault, I must be bad.

Jane, Ian, Jamie and Philip have all been physically abused, hit, burnt, scalded; we hope safe now from more physical hurt but wary, watchful, flitting from person to person, not quite sure how safe they are, who they can trust.

Jane

Jane was a bright lively three-year-old, separated from her mother when a few months old, living with loving foster carers until she was two, while being prepared for adoption to a new family.

However, this went badly wrong and she was physically abused by the adoptive parents. She went back to her original foster carers. Three years old, already having been separated from three families, returned to a family where the adults had told her she was to have a new mummy who would love and take care of her. Nothing is as it seems. When I first met Jane she was lively, controlling everybody around her, constantly talking, using baby talk and a lisp which made what she said fairly unintelligible. She wanted to hit back and control her whole world and she was very angry with her foster carer who she clearly thought untrustworthy, having abandoned her to such monstrous adoptive parents. Obviously, all adults told lies and were untrustworthy. Jane was very angry and determined to be as loud and difficult as possible to get her needs met. If Jane didn't get what she wanted she sat and howled ferociously, but with no tears. This was powerful and hard to resist. I worked with Jane at home with her foster carers to help Jane in her environment. We played together on the mat. Our first play session was chaotic. Jane scrabbling through the toys, testing out the rules and sizing me up and down for signs of weakness. Like many such young children separation of any kind gave her the most difficulty and ending each session was a constant battle, a re-enactment of her distress and anger about all the separations she had experienced.

Even a minor separation was agony for Jane. Would I come again, when was a week later, why couldn't she control me and make me stay? Could she really trust me to come again with the toys? Of course not, all adults tell lies. There were tears when I warned Jane that we had to stop playing. There were screams when we finally stopped. I was firm but assured her I would come again. I said goodbye and was met with a glare and an eloquent shrug of the shoulders.

I returned for the second visit. I was met with an incredulous stare, then the mat was grabbed and play began before I had time to sit. Jane grabbed the baby monkey with a dummy in his mouth:

> 'Is this a story?' I asked.
> 'Yes.'
> 'Shall I write it down?'
> 'Yes.'
> 'How does it begin? Is it once upon a time?'
> 'Yes.'
> 'Right.'

'Once upon a time there was a monkey.'

'Is it a boy or girl monkey?'

'It's a man monkey, and he is very sad because his mummy
smacked him in the bum.'

'What happened?'

'He had a sore bum.'

'What shall we say to the mummy?'

'Naughty mummy. Don't smack the monkey!'

We told the monkey how sorry we were and that mummies shouldn't smack like that. We rubbed his sore bum better and Jane sat him on the chair to watch her play.

Jane then got out the tiny family dolls and the doll's bath and began to play with a baby doll being lowered into the bath which she pretended was filled with very hot water. The baby was slowly lowered into the water, then screamed as her bottom was burnt. Jane was the mother who was shouting at the baby, then played the baby being hurt. Jane played this several times then stopped and put the dolls away. Children often stop play suddenly, as if just realising they have had enough.

Jane was enacting an experience which had happened to her. Playing it for the first time with a listening adult was difficult and emotionally painful. Clearly, Jane didn't know me well, but at least I had come back with the toys as promised and she had the need to discharge anger and distress about her abuse. We expressed sadness for the baby who had been so let down by the grown ups.

We finished with quiet play, making cakes with play dough, nurturing each other with imaginary food. I prepared Jane for the end of play. Again she was angry and refused to stop playing. Again I was firm and we kept the rules. Jane expressed her anger by leaving the room, standing outside and kicking the door, howling her howl of anguish. No tears, just a howl of anger against an unfair world. When I left, I said goodbye, promised I would come again. As before I received the same withering glare, and an indifferent shrug of the shoulders.

On the third visit, Jane greeted me with pleasure. We began to play with the monkey again:

Once upon a time there was a monkey who had a naughty mummy.
She hit the monkey and the baby said 'No don't hurt me'.

The monkey was sat on the chair to watch us play. Before he could watch, he had to acknowledge that he was a hurt monkey. We then repeated the play with the baby and the bath. It was easier this time for Jane to make sense of what was happening to the baby and to be angry with the naughty mummy and say so in the play. She was less aroused and fearful about playing the incident, but the hurt was still painful to recall.

Jane then took the role of the controlling mummy, got out the baby dolls, took my paper hankies and began to wash and wipe the 'babies', blowing their noses and controlling their behaviour. Her handling of the dolls was rough and aggressive.

We finished again with quiet play and Jane managed to leave at the end without too much anxiety or anger. She didn't kick at the door and said goodbye fairly cheerfully when I left. I said I would come again.

By this time life was getting better in the foster home. Jane was talking about her 'naughty mummy' and differentiating between foster mum and 'naughty mum.' In the next session Jane began to play with the family dolls immediately. She didn't want the play with Monkey and went straight into play with the small family dolls. The baby now had a name. She was called Sarah and she was hurt on the leg by Mummy Mary. It was Mummy Mary who hurt the baby; she put hot water on her. As the story is elaborated it becomes less stressful.

Jane got out a little finger puppet of a bee and the baby dolls. The bee then stung the baby dolls on the legs, violently and frequently. The babies were naughty and had to be told off, Jane once again playing the role of the angry mum.

We finished with quiet play with the play dough, not making anything this time. Just regressive play, the tactile sensation of touching and breaking the dough, enjoying the texture and feel of it. The violence of the family relationships played out with the dolls creates the need for regression to re-establish equilibrium. After play Jane said goodbye and left the room quite contained and satisfied.

These were the initial sessions with Jane, when she explored the terrible trauma of being dropped in a bath of scalding water which seriously burnt her. As she became desensitised to this incident, she began to act through experiences of extreme control and discipline which were the norm in her abusing family. These incidents were repeatedly played until the anxiety lessened and her past became less painful for her. Jane also began to differentiate between adults and began to trust a little.

Very young children, given the opportunity to play often, discharge their distress quickly. Young children are inclined to represent their abuse through a simple enactment with toys which closely resemble actual objects. Jane used the toy bath and a small baby doll to represent being scalded in the bath. It is important to have toys which represent household objects that can be used this way. Clearly, information about the abuse incidents is needed if the therapist is to offer appropriate toys.

Jane also needed the monkey which is a rather soft, sympathetic looking object to hold and nurture before she felt secure enough to start her enactment, and the monkey had to be abused before he became a sympathetic observer. I find such soft toys an invaluable comfort for small children who are experiencing distress. The monkey has a dummy in his mouth and seems to represent the vulnerable baby to the child at play.

Jane had nightmares and she began to play about her fear of night and the dark and the safety of her cot. All the abuse she experienced was connected with the adult's desire to prevent Jane wetting herself and wetting the bed. Jane was probably scalded as a threat to prevent her wetting, so she had a particular fear of sleeping in case she wet the bed and would then be punished. She was smacked very hard by 'naughty mummy' if she wet the bed.

Jane used the small family dolls to play about nightmares. She said:

> The baby is in her cot asleep. Naughty mummy comes into her dreams and burns her bum. The baby goes 'aaaaah'. The baby is scared. She says 'Go away you dirty mummy.'

> The dirty mummy smacks the baby very hard in the cot. 'No this is my cot', says the baby. 'You dirty mummy.'

> 'If I shout very loud the Monster will go away.'

This play brought a return of the problem of separation at the end of the sessions. Jane's anger about the control adults exerted over her returned and perhaps if she shouts loud enough the monsters will go away.

There was much repetition of play around the nightmares until Jane felt safer at night. The repetitions lessen the anxiety and the protests at the end of the sessions were less intense. Jane settled into a period of regressive play, wanting the nurture and baby play she missed in her adoptive home. She wanted to go back and explore the world through her senses, to feel safe for a while from the stress of an uncertain future.

She alternated regressive play with expressions of anger at her lack of control over events in her life. In this play she ordered all the baby dolls about and used walking off the mat as a means of telling me that she would play when she chose. Jane's anger with me and her walking off and onto the mat were stylized as dramatic play. She would sit on the mat, fold her arms, tap her foot and make powerful eye contact with me, keeping total silence. Then she would stand and slowly turn, walk to the sofa and throw herself full length and stare . . . and stare! A wholly admirable assertion of her will, and a performance worthy of an Oscar!

There was no more play about the abuse. She had discharged her feelings as best she could and come to an understanding of what had happened in the way a three-year-old can understand. Her nightmares stopped for the time being and she became safe enough to develop the normal interests of any child of her age.

Ian

Ian was a three-year-old boy who came into care because his mother had poured boiling water over his feet and he was constantly physically abused. His feet were badly scarred and he experienced pain when walking. His mother had also neglected him and was unable to meet even the basic needs of nurture. He had been in foster care for some months and was to be adopted.

Ian's speech was difficult to understand as he omitted certain sounds, but he had plenty of expressive language—it was just sometimes difficult to understand his pronunciation. His development was delayed due to lack of stimulation from his mother as well as the trauma of the physical abuse.

He had refused to communicate with his foster carer for two months, but had now begun to talk and settle into the family, although was prone to outbursts of anger. When we began to play together Ian was interested in the mat and the toys, but didn't really know how to play. He found it difficult to understand the boundaries we had made. He took out objects and put them back in the bags. He didn't know what to do with toys. He looked in my handbag, poked at me with his fingers until I reminded him of the rules. Finally he was fascinated by the long witches' fingers in the Monster bag. He put them on his fingers and said 'They burn you'. Then he began to cut and scratch at the toys with the nails. He put the nails back in the bag. I suggested he might like to draw to finish the session and he took out all the pens and managed to draw a scribble for his carer.

At the next session Ian was more contained and settled to go through all the toy bags, still mainly looking at the objects. He was interested in the monsters. He talked a little of monsters who hurt people. I listened. He drew a picture of a bird that could fly and had lots of legs. The bird had purple wings, pink legs and a tail. It was called Mr Bird. We talked about the vast number of legs and why the bird needed so many legs. Ian didn't know.

In the next session he found the wicked witch in the monster bag and told me this wicked witch hurt children's legs. For the next few sessions Ian continued to play with the monsters, making remarks about their cruelty to children. The monsters were very rejecting of each other:

I don't want you. I hate you: I'll cut your willy off'.

And they ate each other up until nothing was left.

After some weeks, Ian began to play with the farm animals and set them out in family groups. He said that all these families of animals had broken legs and fell down and died. The big black bulls didn't get broken but in the end some did. The bulls were trapped together and fenced in so the biggest ones broke the legs of the little ones. The play was quite structured with each group of animals falling down as their legs were broken until all the animals except for some large black bulls were lying down dead from their broken legs. After he had finished the story Ian got out the baby dolls and began to feed them with bottles and put a dummy into his own mouth and mine to give himself the appropriate nurture. Me too, because I had watched the play of the animals.

This play with animal groups went on for several sessions with more and more animals recovering from their broken legs until finally there was only one very weak pony who remained lying on the ground his legs broken but he was still alive. No animals died of their broken bodies, as they had done when Ian began this play. We commented on their capacity to stay alive even with broken legs.

Ian gained confidence after these sessions with the animals and returned to play with the monsters and the witch's fingers. He put the fingers on and sat some little monsters on his hands on top of the false fingers. He said these were naughty monsters who sting people and burn them and put boiling water over them. He scratched and attacked other toys and the image of those grotesque fingers surrounded by monsters clawing and scratching seemed to express for Ian his feelings about his mother and her hands, like some terrifying monster scratching his very body to pieces.

For several weeks Ian's play was about being physically hurt. In each session he took out a variety of toys and the bigger objects ate, beat up, stung or in some way attacked the little objects. We had the crocodile eating babies, the dog bit the rabbit, the horse ate a tree and the bull knocked down the sheep. He made up very short stories:

> Once upon a time there were two little mice and there was a bad cat who scratched the mice, then the police came with the dog and the cat scratched the policeman and bit the dog.

Then he returned to the farm animals. He said:

> Some animals are bad, the horse is a good animal but some horses are good and some are bad. Some horses are dead because the bad horse bit them. All animals fight. There is nobody to rescue them. Some horses run away from the horses that are biting.

We defined running away as a good strategy when dealing with monsters.

After several weeks, Ian's play became less centred on abuse. He chose a wider variety of toys and his play skills increased. There was still a short time in each session when he played about physical hurt, although the play was less intense. At a basic level of understanding Ian was beginning to come to terms with his hurt body. His view of the world from his own experience was that 'All animals fight. There is nobody to rescue them.' We stay with that feeling and find a way to cope. You run away. There is that little choice for Ian. He holds on to that. He is discovering a way to separate from his abuse and the perpetrator.

Ian's behaviour became less aggressive towards his foster carers, his speech improved and he began to make friends at nursery school. His hurt was beginning to heal.

For the older children who were perhaps abused when younger, the actual abuse is lost in the past and yet the legacy of that hurt remains.

Jamie

Jamie, aged eight, had lived with his natural mother until he was six. She struggled to care for him, lost control often and beat him, until finally she beat him so badly that he was taken into care and placed in a foster family. He was six years old.

Jamie was angry with the whole world. He was especially angry with his natural mother for hurting him, but he also loved and missed her. He was angry with his foster mum because she wasn't his real mum. He felt bad, unloved and unlovable, out of control, not sure of the rules of the foster family, because he wasn't sure about rules at all. With his natural mother, the rules changed all the time. He felt powerless, abandoned and abused.

When I first met Jamie for Play Therapy he was excited because he enjoyed playing and drawing and making stories. He had seen me before in the foster home so knew about the mat and play. He wanted some for himself. We did some exploratory drawings and it was clear that he was full of self-loathing, anger and despair. He refused to write his name on his drawings. He told me that he couldn't spell his name and he found it difficult to own to his name. My first task was to help him write and own his name and try to feel pride in who he was.

Jamie's physical abuse had happened some time ago so he didn't want to discharge feelings around the physical hurt. It was the sense of loss, lack of power, anger and jealousy of other children which were the legacy of his past and were damaging his capacity to develop.

So for Jamie our play and his stories were about his lack of self esteem, his sadness about the separation from his mother and how that conflicted with his anger about being hurt by her. He wanted most of all to find a place for himself in the foster family; he wanted to belong, but found himself overwhelmed by his anger about the injustice of his life and that feeling inside just over-ruled the desire to change his behaviour. He wanted to be loving and he wanted to be hating and he didn't know which he wanted most.

As we started to play, he wrote very moral fables, always about a boy called Michael. This is one of his moral fables:

> Once upon a time there was a boy who stole things. His name was Michael. He stole rubbers, pencil sharpeners, money, but worse thing of all was matches.
>
> He lived in a wooden house with his mother and father and the cat.
>
> One day he was playing with the matches he had stolen when a magic devil appeared. He said to Michael 'Light the matches and make a big fire' but just then appeared a fairy with a very loud voice.
>
> 'Stop' she shouted. 'Get away from him devil'. And the little red devil ran away in tears.
>
> The good fairy turned to Michael and said 'You silly boy you could have hurt yourself playing with matches.'

So the boy put the matches away.

The good fairy said 'Next time you want to steal matches say the magic word and that will stop you.'

'What is the magic word?'

'Mollywops.'

So Michael learnt the word and every time he wanted to steal matches he said the magic word.

Jamie's stories were important to him and gave him little strategies to help him control his own behaviour. He was afraid when he was out of control, because it reminded him of his mother when she hit him. His description of the boy in the story who lived in a wooden house defined for him his shaky start in life. Wooden houses and matches are dangerous together and Jamie wanted a bit of 'magic' to help him change. His mother had also burned him with a poker, so fire had powerful meaning.

Jamie liked to repeat his stories or for me to read them to him each week and in this way he managed to curb his stealing behaviour. I must say I didn't identify too well with the good fairy with the loud voice!

Jamie found his anger in the foster family more difficult to change. He knew he was being fostered until an adoptive family was found and he felt like a parcel in transit, not a person. He wrote this story in which the hero is a chocolate, a consumable object. This was the way he perceived himself at that time, as an object, without a name, unloved and unwanted:

There was a chocolate called Michael and every time he went to school he beated up people and he got it on his report and his mother sent him up to bed.

'That's no way for a chocolate to behave especially a Roses Coffee Cream', said his mother.

So Michael climbed out of the window into a tree and fell down and broke his front and he crawled back indoors crying his eyes out.

All coffee cream came out of his front and dripped all over the floor and the dog came up and licked it and Michael said

'Help me please'

and the dog gave him a ride and the mother saw Michael with the broken leg and she called an ambulance to get him to the Chocolate hospital to get coffee cream put in his leg and some chocolate to set his leg.

The chocolate doctor did this and he walked on his leg and kept saying 'Ow' and mum gave him a carry all the way home.

This chocolate wasn't eaten by anybody and he died of cancer when he was 95.

It is interesting how the injury changes during the course of the story, because Jamie was very severely injured on his leg by his mother and this final injury was the one that brought him into care.

'Help me please' cries the Chocolate as the dog licks up his soft centre. But it is a hopeful story, more soft centre is put inside the chocolate who can then walk on the wounded leg set by the doctor and best of all, nobody eats him. His feeling of being an object and being bad was firmly rooted. He wrote another story about Michael which expressed all the things he wanted to do and his fear of the consequences:

Once upon a time there was a boy called Michael and he stole anything he wanted to steal. And he swore. If he wanted to punch somebody he would and if he wanted to kick anybody he would. One day he met the Headmaster and kicked him in the shins. The police arrested him and he went to jail for the rest of his life.

Jamie was struggling with his wish to get even with the whole world of adults in an undifferentiated way. But he had a stronger desire which was for people to care for him. Was he loveable, dare he trust adults? Will that little green devil leave him alone? He had longer and longer spells of settled behaviour when he was loving and gentle and could talk with his carers about his fears before spurts of anger took control.

He began to be able to talk about his situation without losing his temper. When making food with play dough he said:

My mum is a nice lady but she hit me and that's not nice.

But what I feel about her is that she is nice. I feel mixed up. My angry part is like fluorescent pink play dough and my good part green play dough. Red for stop, green for go. My angry part is about being left by my mum, being hit by my mum so I've lost my mum because she hit me.

This is the paradox of abuse by parents and it leaves the child powerless and confused. The initial trauma of the physical abuse has become less important, but the sense of being an object, unlovable, out of control continues and is reinforced in care when a permanent safe place is not found for the child, who seems to be left endlessly suspended, waiting for life to begin.

There is no end in sight for Jamie.

Philip

Philip is ten. He was physically abused by his father when a young child, then physically and emotionally abused by his mother who despised him, constantly put him down and eventually placed him in care. His strategy for coping with this abuse was to deny his feelings. He was busy, cheerful, never angry, lived dangerously for the moment, would go anywhere with anyone, was attached to no one, was attached to everyone, was sad, terrified and lonely. He didn't understand boundaries and rules, he reacted to whatever stimulus was present. He wasn't sure who he was or what he wanted because he was the slave of his parent's anger.

Philip was trying to find his place in a family but it was hard for everyone. The strategies to survive in his natural family—indifference to others, loving everyone indiscriminately, going off on whatever whim takes your fancy—made living in a caring family difficult. It was difficult to keep him safe.

When we first began Play Therapy, Philip played like a five-year-old child and drew like a ten-year-old. We played for many sessions together, Philip enjoying the play but scared of revealing himself. He liked to draw at the end of the sessions and his drawings showed powerful feelings. Philip brought the hopelessness he felt to the play, jumping from one object to another in an attempt to distract. Only now and then did he allow a chink in the armour. He wrote a story about a witch:

> Once upon a time there was a witch called Magna Witch and a boy called Mark was very angry with her because she had turned his little brother into a frog. So he went up to her and stabbed her in the heart, the legs, the arms and the face. 'Ouch' she said, 'I'm going to turn you into a pig' but Mark threw his knife at the witch and it landed into her heart. She died and everyone called Mark a hero and his brother turned back into a boy, but the witch had given him a magic potion and when he turned back into a boy he was only five years old instead of his real age so Mark had to go on a quest for the potion to cure him. He will find it on January 9 1995 and when his

brother takes the potion it will turn him back into his real age but in this case only to seven years old.

You can kill off the witch, but she leaves a legacy behind and however hard you try there is still another problem to solve. The witch appeared now and then in play. She created a variety of spells. She cast spells on trees, turned boys into donkeys for 25 years and generally played havoc with a child's capacity to grow up well.

Then Philip wrote another story:

Once upon a time there was a sad clown and he lived in a dungeon. He wanted to be free but his wife the princess said 'Sorry, I can't let you go'. He starts to scream and then he tries to break away from his chains. Then he gets free and he tries to get her to love him. But no luck, she turns him into a frog, kicks him out and says 'See what you've done. You'll be made into frog stew'. He was angry and he wandered about looking for food. He breaks down the rabbit's door and the rabbit tells him to go away. The frog asks for food and the rabbit says 'yes' and he stays with the rabbit. Then the princess comes and says she is sorry and they live happily ever after and the frog turns back into a clown.

The clown is in prison, gets free, tries to be loved, fails, is rejected, fed, loved, all at the whim of others who never give reasons for their behaviour. The world is a puzzle. Philip wrote on a drawing of himself:

This is a snake path. The life is doomed.

It was important to stay with Philip's confusion. The temptation to tell him how to do things was strong, but he couldn't make sense of consequences or reflect; he could only react and hope for the best. Through his stories we began to ask questions, be thoughtful and to make plans. In 1994 he might make friends, in 1992 there may be fewer arguments. But it's a long way to 1995 when you wake up and discover that inside you are still only seven.

At the time of writing, life is a struggle for Philip. He is beginning to realise that it might be a good idea to think things out, but the rules are still confusing. Anger about his father and the physical hurt have began to emerge. He has not run away from that anger. We continue the journey.

Helping the Physically Hurt Child Through Play

It is important that young children are given the opportunity to understand at the appropriate developmental level what has happened to them when they are physically abused. They need to have a place to discharge their feelings about being hurt by an adult. In this way play can help lessen the lasting effects of posttraumatic stress.

Young children discharge their stress through using objects which closely represent the objects and people involved in their abuse and enact simple reconstructions of incidents. They repeat this play until they make sense of their hurt. Many children do not have the opportunity to discharge their stress after abuse and become confused and angry about what has happened to them.

Older children use symbol and metaphor to play about their physical hurt. If they have had no opportunity to relieve their distress many physically abused children begin to blame themselves. They experience themselves and their hurt bodies as 'bad.' These children need long-term help to give them time to trust the therapist and develop a relationship that will give them the creative space to start to heal.

If children have to be removed from their family for their own safety, stress is compounded by loss of everything familiar to that child. This is painfully expressed in therapy. Some of the themes which emerge for the physically abused child and are played out symbolically are about:

1. The terror of being hurt
2. How the abuse happened
3. Physical pain and disfigurement from the abuse
4. Fear of the perpetrator, love of the perpetrator
5. Loss—of parents, siblings, friends, pets, familiar territory, home/school, my bike, my toys . . .
6. The future—what will happen to me, will anyone love me?
7. Myself—I must be bad, my body is bad,
8. Powerlessness and anger. Nobody listens to me.

Ian, burnt by his mother at two, told the story when playing with slime:

> Slime is blood coming off the face. It bleeds and the hair comes off and you see the blood, and people touch the blood and change into a spider. The blood comes out and spreads all about. The blood all comes out and he was burnt. His mouth opens and the skin cracks.

CHAPTER 6

The Emotionally Abused Child

I was a lonely child. My parents found me difficult, not the child they had wanted. I was too intense, too physically awkward and too quiet for them. My best times were outside with the dogs. Parents want to see themselves passed on in their children. It comforts them to recognise a twist of the head or a way of talking. If there are no points of recognition, if the child is genuinely alien, they do their best to feed and clothe, but they don't love. Not in the transforming way of love (Winterson 1989).

Emotional abuse

Mia Kellmer Pringle (1974) described four basic needs of children for their healthy development. These are: the need for love and security, the need for new experiences, the need for praise and recognition and the need for responsibility.

Emotional neglect occurs when the child's needs are not met. This area of harm to the child is not so easy to define or identify if no other form of abuse is present. If a child is physically or sexually abused, then they are also emotionally abused, but many children suffer neglect of their emotional needs through rejection, humiliation, lack of recognition of their rights as an individual and this can impair their functioning and integrity as a person. Many children physically or sexually abused say that the emotional abuse hurt the most. Constantly humiliated, their attempts to give affection rejected, never praised or recognised, verbally threatened and terrorized they just felt bad, not a real person, part of the wallpaper, invisible.

Peter and Richard were emotionally abused by adults and were finally rejected and abandoned by those adults. Susan experienced multiple abuse from her mother and unknown others—emotional, physical and sexual abuse. She was further damaged in the care system before finding a safe family who fight for her rights and her emotional well-being.

Peter

Peter was five but looked like a three-year-old waif when I met him first at school, where we played together. This was the beginning of a long journey that I was proud to make with him. Peter's mother was an alcoholic who tried to care for him and nurture him, but finally drinking became more important to her and Peter was taken into care. Attempts at rehabilitation with his mother failed because of her drinking problem and at two years of age a permanent placement was sought for him.

Peter was prepared for his adoptive placement and went to a family at three years of age. One year later he was removed from this family because of the emotional abuse he experienced from all members of the family, including the two teenage children. Peter was also hit and bruised by his 'father' but it was the rough handling, and constant humiliation he received from all the family which undermined his sense of self worth.

Back with his foster carers, another adoptive placement was prepared, and Peter met the 'new mummy and daddy'. But before he went to stay, the 'new daddy' rejected him and the placement didn't proceed. So many rejections, hurt and humiliation.

So here we were, having agreed to meet and play at his school. We walked together to the room set aside for our play. He helped me put the mat on the floor. We sized each other up. He seemed to have the face of a seventy-year-old man. He examined all the toys, interested in everything. He took out the monsters and made up a story:

> Once upon a time there was a monster called Peter and a boy called Peter came to visit him and the monster said 'You can't come in' so Peter took a gun and hit him on the head then he shot him and the monster was dead. And good riddance to him. He was a Man Monster.

Then Peter took all the monsters out of the bag and cut them in half or 'shot' them with the toy gun. He took out two sets of Russian dolls, split the mother and father dolls in half and said:

> 'The mother is cut in two and the father is split in two.'
> 'What about the child?' I asked.
> 'No, he is whole.'

Figure 14 - Split in two by abuse

A good ending, was my thought.

Peter finished his play, we folded the mat and he went to the toilet. He shouted to me all the time and asked me to talk back because he was frightened that I would go away while he was on the toilet. I talked, he talked. He came back. I was waiting.

'That was the quickest wee I've ever done' he said. We laughed together, the first of many laughs at our fears and anxieties.

In his first play session, Peter was able to express the hurt he felt at being excluded from a family who had said they wanted him, but had then in the cruellest way pushed him out. In the next session, Peter went straight to the Monster bag and began to cut up the Monsters, and this became a ritual for many months. He played with other objects and ended with the Russian dolls. He took them apart and made up all the smaller dolls. He said they were all him and they were all bad children. Then he said they weren't him but were all people in his family. He turned to me

'All grown ups are bad', he said.

I accepted his assessment as reasonable, in the circumstances.

He spent several sessions playing-out his anger, cutting up monsters, shooting monsters, splitting the Russian dolls in half, making play-dough models of monsters and scrunching them up. I was surprised at the intense ferocity of his feelings—such violence from so frail a body.

We often finished a session with a drawing. He liked to draw himself in a boat, floating between here and there, a constant image for his sense of being suspended, or sailing back to the safety of his foster home.

He read *Where the Wild Things Are* and made up his own story:

> Once upon a time Peter got into a boat and sailed to the land where the monsters lived. He got out of the boat and saw some gorillas and some monsters. And the monsters saw him and said nothing. Peter saw the monkeys and the monsters but he did nothing. So Peter got in his boat and sailed back home into bed.

The sense of paralysis was sometimes pleasant for Peter, rocking in his boat, floating wherever the boat chose to go, but sometimes being powerless was depressing, hopeless. Peter became interested in the snakes as a metaphor for what he expected from the adult world. If all adults were bad, then the best he could hope for was the best bad adult:

> Once upon a time there was lots of snakes and they were poisonous and there was wooden ones and real ones and they were bad. They eat each other, they bite and they whip around and this is what they do whip around and around. They don't speak but they hiss if something hitted them. The crocodile came and bit their tails and Peter came and cut off their tail. There are two good snakes and they liked me but one was bad, so I ended up with the one who liked me and he liked me for ever.'

So the best you could hope for in this bad world full of snakes was to find one who would like you for ever. By this time Peter's social worker had assessed a single woman who was interested in adopting Peter. He was prepared to try again, because he wanted someone special for himself. One picture he drew at this time was a cat:

> This is a cat called Baby. He is very happy because he has lots to eat, a warm bed and lots of strokes. This is his swimming pool.

The pool was empty, waiting to be filled.

Peter met his new carer. He liked her but was wary. He especially liked her father—a grandad at last. A grandad is safer than a dad because he doesn't live in the same house. Peter had his own bedroom. It's safe. Dare he go and live there? He drew a picture of his foster carer's house and he asked me to write his story on the drawing:

> This is a thunderstorm. Mary's house. Everybody is safe inside. If Stephen (another foster child) went out in the storm he might hurt himself. He is in the garden getting wet. He comes back into the

house. Peter didn't go out in the thunder storm. I might get wet but Stephen got his coat on and his hood. I can't do that. If I have to leave Mary's house I'll be scared, but not Stephen.

Peter can leave if it's sunny but not if it's raining. If there is somewhere nice to go, I can leave.

Peter drew another house and a boat sailing away. He wrote:

To Mary.

I can leave Mary's house when it's sunny and I can sail in my boat to the island of England and I'll be happy, because I'll like to lay in the garden of a special house for me. In that house there will be a good mummy waiting for me and I like to see the frogs if there is any there.

His final drawing was his new house:

It was the only house with people. In it there were two faces smiling as they look out of their own windows.

This is Angela's house. I went out in the sun and I played in the garden on my bike and grandad watched me.

There is no snakes.

Peter is settled with Angela, proud of himself and confident in his love for her. She is still Angela; it takes time to trust enough to want another mother. There are no frogs in the garden, but no snakes either. You can't have everything!

Richard

Richard was 14 when we met. He lived in a small children's home where he had been for four years. He was small, agile and wiry, with a wry sense of humour and a sharp intelligence. He could also make me feel incompetent simply by looking at me. We often laughed about this look he had and the way he used it. He said it was reserved for women psychiatrists and therapists. In the 14 years of his life Richard had experienced 19 major moves and had lived with 15 sets of carers, including five different carers in his first year of life. He was born with a hip disability which required five operations and continual hospital visits. The major part of his life so far had been spent with his mother but he had been separated from her nine times. In the first year of his life he had spent seven months with his mother, and the rest of the time with five different sets of carers. Then he had lived with his mother for most of the time from three to nine years old when he was taken into care and went to a foster home. That placement broke down and he went to the children's home when he was ten. Richard's mother had a history of psychiatric illness, having been diagnosed as schizophrenic. Richard had never met his father, who was Scottish.

He was referred to me by his psychiatrist because he wanted to be able to express some of the feelings he had about his relationship with his mother. He was angry about the emotional abuse he had experienced when living with her and while he recognised the reasons for her behaviour he wanted a space to express all the anger he felt about her and have this acknowledged by the therapist.

She had abused Richard emotionally by not being able to bond with him, by being dependent on him, giving him the adult role when he was very small, and subjecting him to traumatic emotional scenes when her own mental state was confused.

The most stressful memories for Richard were of scenes when he was taken into care as his mother was taken to hospital. On these occasions she would cling to him, begging him to do something, he crying and fearful, the policeman or social worker dragging them apart. He said it was a tug of war 'with me as the rope'. These scenes were seared on his memory. The worst time was when he was six. It was four in the afternoon, after school and he felt abandoned as she was dragged off, pleading with him to help her. He was screaming and the policeman was dragging him away. He felt totally responsible for his mother's plight, but was powerless against the strength of the man holding him. He was six, and it was agony.

Richard wanted to explore creative ways of resolving his anger. He didn't want to talk about his relationship, he stated that he wanted to represent it in some way, so he was referred to me. We agreed to ten one hour sessions to focus on the single theme: My mother and why I hate her.

The Sessions

We met together in a small room unfamiliar to both of us. We looked each other up and down and I experienced his 'How to de-skill women' look. I got nervous.

We began with drawing, to find out about each other. He drew the answers to my questions. His best memory of family life was getting his first TV; what he wanted most from other people was friendship, he wanted other people to think of him as generous, loving and funny. The worst memories were the scenes of separation.

I gave him some clay and asked him to close his eyes and think of his mother—think of a feeling he had about her, then mould the clay to shape that feeling. Richard moulded the shape of a castle. I asked him to explain. He said that the feeling was 'let down'. Then he squashed the clay. He said, 'Every time I make a castle my mother destroys it.' We talked about the image of a castle. He told me of his passion for the game Dungeons and Dragons, that he collected the figures, the magazines and the computer games. A castle for him was a special place, a safe place that nobody from the outside could enter.

In the second session, I asked Richard to draw this castle his mother kept destroying. He drew a red castle called 'Cool's Castle'. He described it as boring, strong and fearsome. He wrote a description:

> There was once a castle built with solid walls so nobody could get inside. This was because once in the old days the wicked witch Katherine had destroyed the castle many times so now the castle was impenetrable.

> Inside the castle were precious things, a red gem, Elkhorn the hero and a sword called Heart.

> One day the wicked witch came again and they were fearful in the castle that she might destroy it, so they called in some people from the village to help. But the witch was powerful. Elkhorn came to the battlement and said

> 'You can't come in'.

Richard made a clay model of the witch and destroyed it. He felt that his struggle to separate from his mother and not be destroyed by her was like the story of a powerful myth. I thought about his model of the castle, so easily destroyed by the whim of another and his escape to the world of Dungeons and Dragons where he could enact this power struggle again and again.

I brought a Dungeons and Dragons Magazine for the third session which had an article on different kinds of castles, 'Strongholds Three'. There was a description of three ready-to-use castles for any fantasy campaign. We discussed the merits of each of the castles. One was a robber's castle which was organised like a small village community, another a castle disguised by illusion to seem like a hillside which opened to reveal the castle, and the third was an 'impregnable fortification'.

The Robber's castle was out—too aggressive a place—but the Elf Hill illusion was attractive; magic and illusion have their place, but in the end it was not certain enough in structure to be safe, so we opted for the heavily fortified place. Goldworthy Castle was described as getting its name from the expression, 'worth its weight in gold'. It was designed to be a small, almost impregnable fortification, and all other considerations were subordinated to this purpose. It is the type of castle that would probably belong to a warrior noble, such as a middle-level baron or count. Considering the overall worthiness of its design, it might be a royal castle commanded by one of the king's lieutenants-in-chief or generals.

After the castle was selected, Richard chose all the people he would place in the dungeons. We made some scenes where I played the prisoners pleading to be freed and Richard played Elkhorn, the Lord of the Castle. The prisoners were children from the home where he lived. They were set free after pleading, although one boy with no respect for other people's possessions had a hard time getting free. Two witches, the only adult prisoners, were left in the same dungeon, shackled to the floor. They were both mothers. However much I pleaded, Elkhorn refused to free the two women. They must stay locked away for all eternity, tormenting each other.

I had also brought some drawings of houses and we began to compare houses to castles. In the fourth session we developed the theme of houses from the drawings. Richard created a perfect kennel for some dogs, a tree house for himself aged about 10, a house in heaven and a scary house that everyone is afraid to pass at night.

Richard's kennel for the dogs was a warm, nurturing place with food, warmth, toys, soft cushions to sleep on. The tree house was full of objects: TV, stereo, bed, chair, and nothing else, no food or warmth—that was for the dogs—and all was coloured a uniform brown. Underneath the tree, looking up to the occupier of the tree house was a monstrous woman painted black and green, with her hand outstretched, a grabbing hand.

The house in Heaven was just a door, with a smiling figure blocking the entrance and the scary house was his mother's home with a black door and brown walls. DHS Rules was written on the wall above the door. Houses were not safe places for Richard unless, of course, you were a dog and even the dogs, while nurtured, were not safe and secure.

We returned to the castle and stayed with that metaphor to the end of the ten sessions. Richard wrote a series of sagas about the castle and the kingdom in which the castle was the ruling palace. He had found the creative form in which to express the struggle he felt coping with his early experiences and being let down by his parents, an unknown father and a mother who destroyed that fragile sense of self. How could he survive and separate from that mother?

These are his stories. First, a description of the country.

The Map of the Country, called the Kingdom of the River Town

To the North are mountains where the goblins live. In the West and East are forests where the elves live.

There is a lake and a river which flows to the sea.

The river needs guarding from attack although nobody has attacked the Kingdom from the sea and river.

To the North by the castle is a platinum mine. There are two fields for vegetable growing and there is a great variety of food.

There are livestock.

At the edge of the Kingdom in the South East is a Ogre settlement. They steal the sheep.

The people of the Kingdom live in a settlement of houses guarded on four sides. The houses are guarded by huge walls with gates.

There is no school.

There are 500 people. 300 adults, 200 children.

The people who guard the sheep are wild and strong and are the best fighters in the kingdom. These people are a family of 15 equal participants and they are different from the other people in the Kingdom. The children work in the fields. They have guards when they work in the fields.

The adults run businesses.

There was a house of ill repute.

The date of Elkhorn's Kingdom is 1000.

This is the territory in which Elkhorn's castle is placed. A strong country with some interesting nooks and crannies!

The Castle of Elkhorn

The castle has four gates and guards in the walls.

Tower One is the bedroom, Tower Two is the Armoury, Tower Three contains the Wizard and Tower Four is another Armoury.

The Armouries contain broad swords, swords, spears, crossbows, shields, armour, daggers, mace.

Elkhorn has a magic sword. It is magical and powerful.

He has a shield and armour both very light, magical and studded with gems.

Elkhorn lives with his wife. His mother is banished, she just isn't there.

He has three children. His wife's family are from the people who guard the sheep.

Elkhorn came to rule the Kingdom armed by the old King when he was twelve. He had a great fight with the goblins which lasted a year when Elkhorn was 13. All the survivors went to sea; the old King never returned, he was killed by an arrow.

After the King died Elkhorn's best friend became King for a little while but went out to sea one day and never came back.

The fat general wanted to be King but the people didn't like him. There was a fight at sea between Elkhorn and the General. It was a draw. On the way back the two became friends but a storm came up and the General was thrown off the ship and he drowned because of the weight of his armour.

Then Elkhorn became King.

Richard was very intense when he designed his Kingdom and his Castle and was very clear about the organisation and structure of the kingdom and the castle. The castle tended to be a little bleak when first described but grew more comfortable. He wanted to sort out the organisation of the kingdom to begin the stories and myths of the King of that country. There are three sagas of the Kingdom of the River Town: How Elkhorn Got Rid of His Mother; The War with the Goblins and How Elkhorn became King; The Ogres and How Elkhorn Chose His Wife.

Some of these sagas conflict with the official history of the Kingdom but then that is the way of sagas. Some of the sagas are reported, some told by the great Elkhorn himself.

How Elkhorn Got Rid of His Mother

In 999 when Elkhorn was 14 years of age a sad and terrible thing happened.

Elkhorn was living with his mother in a small hut on the hillside in the kingdom of the River Side.

On June 28 999 at 4pm Elkhorn returned from a walk up the hillside and when he opened the door of the hut he discovered his mother taking part in magic ceremonies. Singing a strange prayer not in any way Christian.

He realised that his mother was a witch. He knew he had to get rid of her, not for himself but for the sake of the townspeople.

He burst into the room, told his mother that he had heard her prayer and that he would have to do something about it.

Elkhorn walked angrily from the hut followed by his mother who was also very angry at being found out. Elkhorn began to run faster and faster away from his mother but she magicked a force field in front of him. Elkhorn realised he was trapped. The only way he could break through the force field was by the power of his anger.

He gathered all the anger in his arms and from the ends of his fingers he shot a magic rainbow which cut through the force field, breaking it in two so he was able to escape.

Then followed a terrifying game of hide and seek through the houses of the town, neither mother nor son sure of what they could do, both wanting but afraid to destroy each other.

They ran away from the houses up to the mountains.

Then Elkhorn felt powerful. He put all his magic into his arms and picked up a huge rock. He threw the rock down, down down the mountain, nearer, nearer his mother till finally it smashed down on her head leaving her unconscious.

As she became unconscious her power over Elkhorn dimmed and he left her to go down the mountain to the castle in the Kingdom where he became page to the King.

When Elkhorn left, his mother gradually regained consciousness and as she raised her head in the dark she saw a troop of goblins coming over the hill.

She stood up, called them and went with them over the hill to their Kingdom and what happened next, my dear, is told in the Sagas of the War with the Goblins.

This was Richard's story about trying to escape from the powerful relationship with a mother. The only escape is through the force of anger and, in fact, Elkhorn can't get rid of his mother; she just goes elsewhere and joins up with other powerful forces.

It was interesting that the time Elkhorn discovers that his mother is a witch is 4 pm, the time when Richard was separated from his mother when he was six.

The War with the Goblins In the Mountains

This story is told by Elkhorn.

My mother was found by the goblins after our terrible game of hide and seek. She became their leader and so began the Goblin War. The war lasted one year.

At that time I was guarding the castle, a page for the old King, and the goblins attacked every day and every night for a year.

One day there was a terrible battle and the King was killed. The shepherds came to help with the battle and Karen, who later became the wife of Elkhorn and her five brothers took part in the slaughtering of the goblins.

As Karen and her brothers went through the army ranks of goblins, Karen came upon a woman leading them. This woman said some magic words and the brothers dropped their swords and fled. But Karen stood her ground and charged her. Her sword broke against the witch's staff, then a goblin came up behind Karen and tried to kill her, but Karen killed the goblin with her bare hands and took his sword. She thrust it in the mother's stomach then chopped her head off.

This act ended the war of the Goblins because Karen brought my mother's head on a staff. It was bloody and mangled and on seeing the head the Goblins ran away.

My mother was dead. I didn't realise it was her because she was so disfigured.

When the King was dying he turned to me and said,

'You will be the next King because I have no children and you are the loyalist and fairest of my men'.

Years later, when I found out that my mother had been killed, I cried, because she was my mother and although at times she was evil, she was still my mother.

Interestingly, this story was written in the first person and the female person/part that manages to slay the mother does so in ignorance and so there is no blame. At the end of the story Elkhorn owns his mother and mourns her.

After Richard had written this story his attitude towards his mother changed. He began to separate from her, not by disowning her, nor by being angry, but by becoming an individual in his own right. He began to speak with her yet keep their lives separate and make his own boundaries that were boundaries and not fortifications.

Then he wrote the third story.

The Ogres and How I Chose My Wife

After the battle with the Goblins there was peace only for a short time.

The Wild Shepherds and Karen went back to their villages to discover that the Ogres had been visiting—stealing and killing sheep, burning the huts and killing the villagers who were left to tend the sheep.

The Wild Shepherds returning from the war had a big fight with the Ogres. Elkhorn was to bring the palace guards to assist the Shepherds but he came too late. The Shepherds won the battle but Karen was angry with Elkhorn. 'You're worthless' she said.

However, Elkhorn was determined to prove her wrong. He stayed with the Shepherds and got them new sheep from the Elves. The chief of the Wild Men was so pleased with the help that he gave Elkhorn permission to marry Karen.

They married the same day and there was a huge feast and a huge celebration and everybody was happy.

For many years from that time there was peace in the Kingdom and even the knowledge of how his mother died didn't spoil the love between the King Elkhorn and Queen Karen.

The children of the King and Queen grew up happy and content, and on the death of King Elkhorn his son became King and ruled long and wisely. He always said his wisdom came from his mother and father who had given him the happiest of childhoods.

This final saga, written in the third person like the first story, defines a future for Elkhorn when he is separated from his past miseries and a person in his own right. Lessons are learnt and the children became wise through the love of their parents.

Richard was satisfied with the stories. He had actually created a history and was proud of his skill. The anger fell away and chinks appeared in his fortifications. He had time to spend on the joys and problems of adolescence. He let his mother go with love and compassion.

Susan

Susan is a chaotic child who has experienced a totally abusive beginning to her life and, as with most abused children, cannot just be neatly categorised as sexually, physically or emotionally abused.

I first met Susan when she was four years old. She was living with a foster family in an intermediate placement prior to an adoptive family being found for her. She had been lost in the care system for two years and nobody was quite sure what had happened to her other than she had been physically abused by her mother, who had hit and thrown her about.

The foster family were shocked by the disorder of her behaviour. She was a child in chaos, her life a confusion of experiences of which she could make little sense. She had, however, found a family who cared about her, were puzzled by her behaviour but wanted to help her. They have held on to her now for three years and will continue to care for her a day at a time for as long as possible.

Susan loves them, is attached to them and they are her family. They are a deeply caring, committed family who have fought long battles for Susan to make sure she has the most appropriate care and schooling. The family have made great sacrifices, feel they have to learn much, often think they are mad to take on such a task, but on they go.

Susan had been taken into care at the age of two after her younger brother had been so physically abused by his mother that he was brain damaged. He had subsequently been adopted and Susan was placed in a children's home for two years. Then she was placed with her foster carers who found they had a little girl who was totally out of control and chaotic in her responses to care and nurture.

It was difficult to sort out the origins of her behaviour or to find out much about her early life. I began Play Therapy with her in the foster home and saw her for three years, once a fortnight.

Not therapy? It's free play (handwritten annotation)

The first Play Therapy session with Susan was an expression of her chaos, confusion and fear; she was trying to function and make sense of a world she didn't understand. Everything spilled out in an enormous splurge of feeling. She grabbed toys, got over-excited, talked gibberish, spat, swore, then finally began to play with the baby dolls. She hit the doll and said her brother had killed the baby. We will take it to the doctor's to be mended. I was the doctor. Then the baby doll had its head bitten off by the crocodile puppet and had to be taken to the doctor's to be mended. Susan said that the baby was beaten all over and especially between the legs and there was blood everywhere. I had to mend the baby, putting cream on the wounds. We ended the session as it had begun, in utter chaos, toys flying, spit spitting, and a choice variety of sexual posturing. Endings were intolerable; how could she trust me to come back?

In the second session, Susan began the play with the dolls again, sending them to the doctor to be mended. Throughout the play she again talked in gibberish, shrieked, rolled about on the mat, spat on the mat and dripped saliva on to the mat. When the end of the session drew near and I told Susan she could only play with one more thing before we must stop, she began to hide the toys. She then hid some small toys in her knickers and stood up and shouted 'fuck me' for several minutes, bending over and dancing in a sexualised way, advancing towards me. I told Susan I wouldn't touch her in any way and eventually she relaxed and removed the toys. We talked about grown ups who had hurt her in this way and that nobody here wanted her to play that way. She was puzzled.

In the next session Susan developed the play with the doll. It represented her brother, she dropped him and hit him and he died. She repeated this play again and again. It was clear through her play that she thought she had killed her brother by dropping him. She was sure her brother was dead. In fact anybody who left her was 'dead', which to Susan meant that you would never see them again and it was always her fault. So you tried to keep them from 'dying' by hiding their things, or offering them something 'rude', which Susan thought all adults wanted.

I explored the injury to her brother with the social worker and discovered that her mother had blamed Susan. In fact Susan was told that she had killed her baby brother. The police had also been told that Susan had dropped her brother and that that was what had caused his injuries. It was quite clear from the injuries that this was not the case and Susan's mother finally admitted to throwing the baby across the room.

Susan was two years of age at the time, but had accepted the blame for her brother's injuries and because she hadn't seen him since and nobody had told her what had happened to him, she had assumed that he was dead.

This emotional abuse had so affected Susan that it took some time for her to understand that her brother was alive. Susan's foster carers helped her and she began to express anger about what grown ups had done to her. The emotional abuse she had suffered from her mother was compounded in the care system where for two years nobody had thought to explain to her what had happened to her brother. Her rights to information about her family were abused, so she suffered further pain and loss and most of all carried the burden of guilt, thinking she had killed her brother. She didn't have much energy left for the ordinary pursuits of curiosity and learning.

The chaos in play continued, but each session subsequently had some strands of ordered play surrounded by chaotic play and bouts of swearing and sexual enactment. The chaotic play diminished in time and gradually we began to tease out various themes which were causing Susan great distress. We were able to address these issues to help her make some sense out of the events she had experienced.

Susan visited her brother and his adoptive parents and so came to understand that she hadn't hurt him and that he was alive and with a family, as she was. She made up this story soon after:

> Once upon a time there was a black and white pig called Susan who gave a birthday party.
>
> She was five. All the monsters came but they were good. Tom came with his new mum and dad and my foster mum and her family.
>
> The pig made the biggest cake in the world, she got the biggest piece, Tom got the second biggest piece.
>
> The pig wanted to look after Tom but he needed a new mum and dad. There is no blood on his head now.

Susan wanted to do something about the anger she felt towards her mother, so her foster carers and new social worker arranged a visit to the local Police Child Protection Unit where she was able to tell the police what her mother had done and the police officer was able to explain what he had done when her brother was hurt. Susan's voice was heard and what she had to say was acknowledged as serious by the police and she began to let go of some of her anger. The sexual play diminished in time, although not before some embarrassing enactments with male shop window dummies when the family were out together. Susan still has difficulty controlling her sexual behaviour, but it is lessening at the moment.

Susan made up stories to sort out her behaviour:

> Once upon a time there was a witch who was nice but sometimes she did silly things like stealing toys and stealing from the tuck shop at the witch's school.

> Sometimes she wet herself and shit herself and sometimes when she felt very very bad she put shit on the wall. It was so smelly. The witches said,

> 'Why are you doing that you silly witch? We all love you. We don't think you're bad so clean up the mess.'

> So the witch cleaned up the mess and decided she would never put shit on the wall again.

As she began to make sense of rules and to feel loved, so Susan began to control endings better. She realised she didn't have to offer me a piece of herself to persuade me to return. She began to understand that goodbye didn't mean that you had killed the person who left. She discovered that she didn't have that power, which was a relief.

When the therapy finished we said our final goodbye. This was the first ending shared and agreed by both parties. Susan and I both decided that she had sorted out enough about her early life and she could learn how to do things with her foster family; she had spat enough, said enough rude words, been angry enough and could stop all that if she really thought about it.

Susan tells her friends that she doesn't see me any more because she feels better now. She also knows that I see other children at the time I used to see her, so the fact that I have left doesn't mean I have died. It is important to give children some image of what the therapist might be doing when they no longer visit.

For Susan's foster family, there are good days and very bad days; the progress is slow. Sometimes for the foster carers it's a treadmill. Some days she can't contain the spitting, the smearing, the anger, but slowly there is change. The role of the therapist was to tease out what Susan's concerns were and support the family, who had the major role of caring for her. The whole change in Susan came about through the love and devotion given to her by her carers; the whole family, but especially her foster mother. This work could only be undertaken with a child in a secure, loving environment, sharing the work with the carers who take the brunt of the constant chaotic behaviour. Clearly, other constructive help is also needed for such a chaotic child and an acknowledgement of the difficulties and practical help to the family who care for her. Respite care and support is essential for the family.

As a therapist, I can only admire those families who go on caring for damaged children, who change so slowly and whose damage can never be fully repaired. It seems a strange world where money can be found for expensive residential placements for damaged children, but no offers of support, help and therapy for children who might be able to live in a family if this extra support was available.

Perhaps I should end with one of Susan's stories. Throughout the time I played with her, America was the place which represented the perfect world. She had been there on holiday with the foster family. Susan thought it was the most wonderful time of her life. For the family, it was a nightmare. This story is a metaphor of life with Susan. Susan took the small family dolls and put them in the car:

> There's no petrol in daddy's car. Oh it's starting to go.
>
> Miss Puggy Pug is in the car. She wets her pants. She just sits in the car and does nothing else. She doesn't play willies. She ain't that rude. Only a little bit rude.
>
> Miss Puggy Pug got no mummy and daddy. Does poohs in her pants. That's why no mummy and daddy. Going to America. Where are you going?
>
> None of your business fat pig.
>
> It's gonna be a long journey.

I can't but agree with Susan:

> 'It's gonna be a long journey.'

CHAPTER 7

The Sexually Abused Child

> It is well known that all ogres live in Ceylon and that all their beings are contained in a single lemon. A blind man slices the lemon and all the ogres die (Indian Antiquary, 1872).

Much of Play Therapy with young children who have been sexually abused consists of trying to contain in play those Ogres who abused the children, and help the children understand, in an age-appropriate way, what has happened to them. The purpose of the journey is to find a safe place for the survivors and a place to put the Ogres. Play Therapy is used as part of a treatment programme for sexually abused children, not as part of the investigative procedures.

Children who come for Play Therapy experience a variety of problems associated with their sexual abuse, notably nightmares and sleep problems, feelings of guilt and worthlessness, sexualised behaviour, difficulties at school, inability to make friends with their peers, feeling lonely, isolated, different, a general sense of being an object not a person.

Children need direct information about what has happened to them. Help about their body boundaries, what are good touches and bad touches, how they can tell someone about bad touches. They need age-appropriate sex education to help them put their sexual abuse in a context. And they need Play Therapy which gives children the space to come to terms as best as possible with the stress and loss experienced through sexual abuse. It is important to help children to repossess their bodies and find an identity not wholly bound up in their past abuse.

Young children who have been sexually abused experience a monstrous invasion of their whole being. At a time when children begin their first faltering steps, starting to explore what is 'me' and what is 'not me' sexually abused children are being engulfed in an overwhelming physical experience with an adult or adults which is incomprehensible and undermines their whole sense of being a separate physical person. It is very difficult for children to develop their own separate identity and cope with sexual abuse and the manipulations of the abuser.

Sarah, aged six, told me she felt as though she was being squashed until she couldn't breathe when her grandfather lay on top of her on the bed. She was frightened and didn't understand what he was doing.

Amanda, aged five, said she felt she was choking and she couldn't breathe when her daddy put his willy in her mouth and she had to swallow white stuff. Sometimes when she swallowed food she felt that funny feeling again, as though she was choking.

Wendy, aged five, told me her uncle asked if he could sleep in her bed. She said:

> He promised he wouldn't wee all over me if I said yes but he always did. If I don't let him sleep in my bed he shuts me in the attic for ages and ages and it's dark and I'm scared.

These young children felt betrayed, tricked, guilty, ashamed, and yet aware of having a sort of power over adults which they couldn't understand and didn't want. It is inevitable that children who are sexually abused are emotionally abused, being threatened or manipulated by adults for their gratification, which disregards the children's needs. Young children don't necessarily understand that they have been sexually abused, not having adult concepts about sex. However, they do know when they are hurt and made powerless or have experienced a relationship which is engulfing, frightening and confusing.

Some young children are threatened if they tell and forced into sexual acts, others seduced, eroticised, sucked into relationships to become a sexual object to satisfy the needs of the adult.

Wendy's father said he would slit her throat if she told anyone about what he did. He also said he would slit the throat of the person she told. Sarah was told she would be responsible for members of her family going to prison if she told anybody. Setting up a therapeutic alliance with these two children took time, before they felt safe enough in the relationship.

Wendy slit doll's throats with a knife for many weeks, observing my reactions, testing my capacity to cope. She felt responsible for her own safety and for my safety. She had to test out my capacity to face the threats from her father before she could trust me, and she had to know me very well before she could tell me about her father's threat towards me, in case I couldn't cope and left her. I had to make it clear to Sarah that I would inform her social worker if she named any perpetrators during the time we played together and she accepted this, knowing that she could choose to remain silent. The intention of the therapy was to help her, not to find out information about the abusers. We bounded our relationship in this way. Her sadness is about loneliness, her inability to make friends and her desire to control the world, as she feels out of control of herself. We play through those themes and, for the time we are together, she is in control of her play and some of her anxiety lifts. She has even dared to admit that she misses the relationship with her grandad and the power it gave her to control him. She feels scared because she tries to make friends with other children by exerting her power and they don't respond like grandad.

Sarah wrote a story about her sense of herself:

> There was once a big hairy pink snake and it could talk and move, and one day it met a little girl and ate her all up. When she came out of his tummy she was a monster snake too, and she gobbled up people and she turned into a pig.

> This little pig didn't want to be a pig but didn't know how to turn into a girl, and she doesn't know what to do.

This is a common theme with young children—the abuse turns me into a monster and how can I return to being a child?

When very young children are sexually abused and show sexualised behaviour such as masturbating in public, or being flirtatious, they are doing what they have been taught to do. Many adults find this behaviour very confronting in a young child and sometimes get angry with the child in a way which reinforces blame. So the child thinks 'I must be bad if adults get so angry with what I do'. In this way we constantly re-abuse children by reinforcing their sense of shame. Our anger should not be pushed onto the child, however confronted we feel.

Many young children suffer the loss of their family after the abuse is discovered and again the child thinks that they must be bad and to blame for what happened. As one child said:

> It's my fault, if I hadn't had a body then my daddy couldn't hurt me and we'd still be together.

This sense of 'being bad' shows through the behaviour of the child.

Wendy would wash her hands for half an hour after a visit to the toilet and use most of the toilet roll before she felt clean.

And Tony wrote:

There was once a boy called Weirdo who was different. His brain fell out of his head, he had one blue thumb and one red thumb and he had lots of red lumps on his hands.

The other children thought he was weird because he looked different but inside he was the same as everyone else.

Cultural values about sexual abuse can add confusion and distress for young children because of the pressure on the parents from within their cultural community, particularly if the group is small. But it is also important for the therapist to recognise what are genuine cultural differences and what is being used as an excuse to deny the abuse of the child. Sometimes, in families of different racial mixes, the abused child rejects people from the racial group of the abuser, which causes family conflict and racial conflict. Children need help to clear this distortion.

Many young children love the person who abused them and experience conflict and confusion about loving and hating the same person, having such powerful reasons to hate. Wendy used to say:

'I still love Kevin you know.'

'Of course you do, he's your father' I said. 'But he did things to you that grown ups shouldn't do to children. If he came in here I'd smack his bottom'.

Wendy laughed. 'Oh you are funny Ann'.

Having it acknowledged that her father was loveable, Wendy could go on to say that Kevin had done some really bad things, but she felt she couldn't talk about the bad things until I had accepted that she loved him too. After all, to deny good in your own father is, for the young child, to deny good in themselves.

These are some of the conflicts and anxieties which young children bring to the therapist. Some children are unable to speak much of the horror they endured but manage to draw and play. The therapist is the empathic listener, acknowledges the nature of their experience and the conflicts it brings.

The Difficulties of Young Children

Mary

Mary was five when she was referred for Play Therapy. She had been sexually abused by her uncle and had disclosed this to her mother. The family had coped very well with the stress of her abuse but it had split the extended family apart and changed everybody's lives.

Mary was having difficulties with sleeping; she wouldn't sleep in her own bed, wanting to sleep with her parents, and she had terrible nightmares. She became anxious if separated from her parents for any length of time. Her play was about a monster, a huge green monster, bigger than anybody else in the whole world and it gobbled you up. It did rude things to little girls and especially licked people.

We decided the only way to combat this creature was to turn Mary into Super Ted in her nightmare so that she could fly high up and away and avoid being caught and swallowed by the green monster. Flying was the best strategy because the monster was so huge.

Mary managed to dream of changing into Super Ted but she still seemed to be distressed about this green slimy monster. We made the story of the nightmare again and I asked her if she missed some of the monster's licks and she said she did. She described the erotic feelings she had about the monster. She found these feelings overwhelming, but we found the best way to sort it all out was to use the puppets to enact these touches. She said that at home she played those touches with her dolls. We thought that was a good way of dealing with those feelings. Once Mary had her sexual feelings accepted she began to feel less overwhelmed by them. She had been afraid of her abuser, but overwhelmed by the physical touching. As she played with her dolls and the puppets and I assured her that lots of children felt the same way, she felt less of a monster herself and the play eventually ceased.

Mary still found it difficult to separate from her parents but gradually began to sleep on a single bed in their bedroom until she dared go back and sleep in her own room again. It was over a year before she felt confident to do this and to stay in school for the whole day without the support of her mother.

The family were patient and supportive over Mary's distress and coped with her feelings and their own distress at seeing their child changed by the abuse. Surrounded by this love and care Mary grew more confident as time passed.

Sally

Sally was eight years old, abused by her brother who was eighteen. This abuse has gone on for many years until she was able to tell her parents.

Her brother was removed from the family and the parents supported Sally's need for therapy.

Sally was cheerful and outgoing, worked well in school and to all appearances is a pleasant, normal child. However, she has frightening nightmares and feels angry and violent about the abuse and the length of time she suffered. Her brother threatened to beat her up if she told and she lived in fear of his threatening behaviour. Her childhood was over-shadowed by the power her brother exerted over her.

Her stories are about a king, queen, princes and princesses. There is one bad brother who harms all the children, especially the babies:

> The children all go to bed and they all sleep in the same room. There is a horrible bossy brother, he is nine and big and bossy. This big brother is nasty and rude to the little girls. He stops them telling mum by saying 'If you tell mum, I'll punch you.'

> The bad brother sneaked into the babies room and he was rude. He told the babies 'do as your brother says or you go into care'.

Sally's stories about this family are about boundaries of behaviour, who sleeps where, how to protect yourself, what you can demand for yourself. One of the young babies who might get abused by the bad brother takes a dog to the room and the dog barks to warn the baby that the bad brother is on the prowl. If only in play Sally is learning strategies to keep herself safe.

When Sally draws pictures of herself and her brother she draws a head and a vagina as herself and a head, a penis and testicles for her brother. She draws her brother without and with pubic hair and this defines the length of time she was abused by him. John with and without pubic hair delineates her childhood. Some of the violence Sally feels is expressed in her stories. She made a huge monster out of slime and said:

> This monster bite the little girl and gets all blood out of her. He's a rude ghost, swearing and saying 'fuck off' to the little girl.

> The little girl is lying underneath him. She punches him in the mouth and it's bleeding.

> The monster has got a big horrible tongue and two mouths. He said 'ouch' because I broke his body.

> The little girl punches him in the privates because he was being dirty with the little girl. She punches him in the leg so he can't walk. His privates are hanging out.

The monster punches the little girl. She says, 'Help, help, no, no'.

There are many such expressions of fear and violence and horrific descriptions of her abuse in violent dehumanised stories. The abuse has left this child with the impression that her whole body is about sex; just a 'hole' for sex. For small children these images of a 'hole' a 'slit' and a 'tent' occur often—a 'hole' in which to drop slime, a tent through which people walk, a tent full of 'poo'.

In the complex and tortuous journey we make together, Sally and I explore how to find a body and a self which she can keep safe from further abuse, to confirm that she is a person in her own right, not just a piece of flesh for the gratification of others.

It is sometimes difficult to see a way through the horror for a child like Sally. But she is hopeful, so we begin to find delight in small pleasures. I try to find comfort:

> Even in the dark, a fire burns in the distance. Long years the hearth-keeper keeps his silence, lightening the dark, leading children home. There is food for the hungry, rest for the weary. Warm and light is the fire. Along the road life's children sing. Voices join in the darkness. This is a beginning (Trans. Ellis 1988).

Children with Learning Difficulties

Children and adolescents with learning difficulties can find it very difficult to make sense of their experience or talk about what happened. So play is a powerful medium for healing and understanding.

Sophie

Sophie was fourteen years old; she had moderate learning difficulties and went to special school. She had been long-term fostered with the same family for fourteen years. She was happy in her foster family and saw her natural mother often. She was safe and secure, knew her natural mother couldn't look after her, but enjoyed meeting her. However, school was a different matter. I was asked to see Sophie to help her sort out her school difficulties. She was afraid to go to school and said the boys were 'rude'.

Sophie enjoyed play. She was delighted to see all the variety of toys and amazed that she could play with anything she wanted. She liked the idea of sitting on the mat where she could say what she liked, because she had confused ideas about what she called 'rude' things. She had listened to conversations of other adolescents in her group about sex, but was unsure what it meant.

In the first session, after enjoying an exploration of all the toy bags, Sophie began to draw and talk about herself. She felt she was a very bad person; she hated school so much she wanted to kill herself.

It was clear from her play and drawings that Sophie was being physically abused and bullied into participating in inappropriate sexual behaviour at school. She was eventually removed to a small tutorial unit. However, this took time. Her foster carer had fought long and hard about Sophie's placement at school, having been anxious for several years. As is always the case with sexual abuse, there was much anger, denial and blame from adults involved and this made Sophie even more depressed, although she gained strength from her foster carer.

The early work with Sophie was to help her make sense of the sexual abuse to which she was subjected. Play, drawing and information about body parts, ways to keep safe and information about sex. She had been told some amazing ways of getting pregnant by other children in her group and was worried. The abuse she had experienced was to do with inappropriate touching of genitals and being forced to masturbate the boys. Much of Sophie's anxiety was about the false information she had been given about sex and the general as well as the sexual bullying she experienced at school. Much of her depression lifted when she left school.

Sophie's confusion about her life and what had happened to her at school was expressed through drawings and stories about paths and mazes. Her first drawing of a path of her life was very depressing. She drew a path and at the top of the path a drawing of herself, then further down a drawing of herself and her mother saying goodbye, then the school building like a prison crossed out, then herself and a companion then nothing on the path until a drawing of Sophie dead and she wrote, 'I am dead I was killed by a knife, killed by a bad man.' She drew another path and wrote 'nothing between life and death'. She drew a flower and wrote 'It is dead'.

She told me that this is what she felt her life would be like. Sophie began to play to sort out her confusions. Once she felt safe from the abuse and began to understand the meaning of sex from information given to her, she became more confident about herself. Her drawings showed optimism.

The maze became alive. Sophie is sitting in the centre of the path enjoying herself picking flowers, the only monster present being a young man who liked her who she was able to reject because she didn't like him. She wasn't bullied by him, or afraid of rejecting him. He is still a monster, of course, but one she can do something about.

Sophie has periods when she feels confident, but the old feelings come back if she has a lot of stressful encounters. She tries to remember the rules, but sometimes in her excitement she forgets and finds she can't cope. She wants to be safe, but she wants to explore the world, so it's a step at a time.

Tina

Tina was eight years old when she disclosed abuse by her uncle while away from her mother at boarding school. Tina was returned home to her mother. She then disclosed that she had been further abused by boys at boarding school but now she was safe with her mother who had broken all contact with her abusing brother.

I worked with Tina and her mother and, while Tina played, her mother watched and followed up any suggestions I made to help Tina. Much of the work, again, was task-based to help keep Tina safe from further abuse by learning about body boundaries. Most of the work was done by her mother, who was very conscientious and kept Tina very safe without making her feel bad.

Initially, Tina explored some of her experiences of abuse through simple play and, after several months, she became more settled and began to gain in self confidence. She enjoyed her new school and felt safe at home with her mother. Both Tina and her mother are rightly proud of the progress they have made to heal the hurt. Tina's mother has sensible advice which she now gives to other parents who find it helpful because they know it comes from direct experience. It is important to help parents to help their own children in these circumstances. The therapist can show the mother ways of helping their child and give them information about appropriate books and toys. We empower the child when we help the parents.

Sexually Abused Boys

Boys who have been sexually abused experience the same feelings of anger, sadness, low self esteem, confusion and loss as girls. As with girls, most boys are abused by men. Some boys feel anxious about their sexuality having been abused by a man and there is an ambivalence about hating their own sex. Boys also express their need for revenge by wanting to do the same as their abuser and the therapist may have to deal with the child as victim and perpetrator. This also applies to girls, who can take their revenge in a variety of ways.

Bolton et al state:

> No perfect correlation exists between previous victimization and future perpetration; suggestions do exist that there is some relationship (Haynes 1985).

> The link between childhood sexual victimization and subsequent aggressive sexual behaviour by adolescent or adult sex offenders is posited by the literature (Groth 1979). It has also been proposed that children of parents who were child sexual abuse victims may be at some increased risk for sexual victimization and abuse of sexuality. These hypotheses find predominant support in theories which suggest that victimized children become victimizers in an attempt to masterthe trauma of their own experiences and take on the power that the adult victimizers held over them (Bolton, Morris, MacEachron 1989).

Alan

Alan was five when I met him. He had been sexually abused by his father, who was now in prison. Alan's parents were unable to keep him safe from further abuse so he was in care, waiting for an adoptive family, when we met. Alan was nervous, quiet, and afraid to make eye contact, but he liked to play. In the first session, he played with all the toys, to find out what I had and his favourite bag was the one containing the heroes and monsters.

In the second session he went straight to the monster bag and began to play with a monster toy with a large rubber face and big mouth with a large tongue. Alan said:

> The monster's opening his mouth. He said 'hello' He said 'willy'. Now he's opening his mouth. He's licking me with his tongue.

Alan put the monster down. He made a 'family' with the snakes, then he shot them. He played with a toy frog and pretended it was eating a worm. Then he put the monsters away.

He took out the play dough and began to make food with precise, careful movements. He took out the puppet crocodile. He made cakes for me with the play dough, spaghetti for himself and willy chips for the crocodile. The he made 'hard willy sausages' and said that the crocodile's dad made him eat willies.

I asked if it was a story and I wrote down what Alan made up:

> Once upon a time there was a crocodile whose dad made him eat willies. This made the crocodile very bad-tempered so he bit lots of people. One day, somebody, a boy, made him willy chips.
>
> He had a friend called Bear and the boy made nice cakes for Bear who ate it all up then went for a little sleep.
>
> Then Crocodile ate the willy chips and he died and that was the end of the Crocodile. The boy had made himself nice food and ate it all up.
>
> The End.

Alan looked at me throughout the telling of the story to test out my reaction. He was much concerned with 'good' food/nurture and 'bad' food.

In the next session Alan got out the monsters again and set about shooting them. He made them blind by shooting them in the eyes. He picked all the animals to shoot in this way. The toy frog has a pair of glasses and Alan took them off, saying that you take your glasses off when you do naughty things. Alan made up another story:

> Once upon a time there was a rude monkey called Michaelangelo. He kept showing his willy to children and that was naughty. So one day the frog swallowed the monkey's willy and ate it all up. Then the frog died.

Alan enjoyed that story. He took out the crocodile puppet and continued:

> Once upon a time there was a crocodile who loved chips. He loved them so much that he eats them off the floor. One day he ate so many he got fat and when he tried to swim he was too fat but he could float. He can float anywhere he wants to go and he dreams about turtles and his lake which is his home.

I was assured that these chips were ordinary chips not willy chips. Alan's need for love was strong at this time; he could never get enough, never be satisfied.

Alan had dreams about being nurtured, but nightmares about his abuse. His next story expresses this well:

Once upon a time there was a witch that flew on the back of a snake and she bit Ann's eyes out. She went blind. She cried 'Help, help, I want to see' so the snake threw her eyes back.

There was a frog who ate a fish but if somebody held his legs he couldn't eat.

The turtles killed Michaelangelo trying to find each other. I caught Donatello. I didn't want him to get killed. You might get slimed and die. The snake hissed at my feet being rude. Shredder fell and broke his leg, hopping. Spider came and ate Shredder. Spider begins to lick the Turtles. It's nice not rude.

I got blind then. Ann gave me my eyes back.

Then Alan got out the small family dolls and placed a family of mum, dad and two children in the car. He picked up a toy helicopter and hit the car with it. He said:

They are dead. They are all blinded by the bonnet of the car.

Alan felt confused, lost from the rest of his family, waiting to find adults who could love and care for him, abandoned, abused, afraid, his life blighted by the abuse and the consequent loss of family.

A boy who lived in the same foster home as Alan had found a new mum. Alan came to the next session feeling vulnerable. He took out the monsters and played again about the monster who ripped out eyes. He said:

This monster eats eyeballs, bottoms, and willy glasses so I had no eyes, no body and no nose.

Then he made a snowman out of play dough. He had a red head, a green tummy and yellow legs. Alan said that he was nice. He continued to play around the abuse and how he felt eaten up, blinded and poisoned. He interspersed this with nurturing play and stories about his consuming need to be nurtured and loved. Then a family was found for Alan and he began to visit. He was thrilled—excited, but very scared. He wrote this story:

Ann is scared of ghosts, especially green bogeys because they cut your head off and scare Ann.

This is Alan's house. It is red with just me and Raphael, the Turtle. We make our own food and drink, we don't speak to anybody. It's not safe in the house. There's too much ghosts. Green slimy ghosts like Slimer and he eats me up and Raphael. The house is empty but we dropped out of Slimer's tummy and ate him up and he is in our tummy now. But the house is still not safe.

He was afraid to go forward because he still felt haunted by the ghosts of his past. Eventually, the house got safer and Alan moved on to his new family. We go on together; it will take time.

Colin

Colin was ten when I first met him. He was at boarding school because his mother had neglected him and his local school couldn't cope with his behaviour. He went home to his mother every other weekend and he felt a great loyalty towards her.

Colin was referred by his social worker as being in need of therapy because the police had discovered a sex ring organised by adolescent males in the block of flats where Colin lived. He had admitted to the police that he had twice been sexually abused by one of this group, a fourteen year old boy called Smith. It was felt that Colin had been traumatised by this experience and there were some concerns that he had recently been interfering with some young children himself.

Colin had to go to court as witness and he was terrified of seeing Smith. It was difficult for Colin at this time to think of anything but his fear of meeting Smith in court. In our play Colin made it clear that the events which terrified him the most were about physical violence. This fear was long standing and had begun when he had witnessed the physical violence of men friends towards his mother. One man in particular, now in jail for murder, had terrified him. There had been lots of fights, punch-ups and knife fights but on one occasion the fight was about Colin, and he had stood in the room paralysed, watching the knife slash his uncle's arm, waiting for his turn. Colin stood there, not existing, with no will, no determination, just becoming part of the wallpaper.

At the last minute, Colin didn't have to appear in court because Smith changed his plea to guilty, so we could begin therapy without the weight of the court appearance hanging over us. In the playroom, I asked Colin to make a path to walk on, which he called the path of life. I asked him to stop on the path at the time when the sexual abuse started, tell me his age and what happened. He stopped on the path at the age of four and described what happened.

He said it took place in Smith's bedroom. There were usually four boys present. Smith made you take your pants off and lie on the floor.

Smith touched your genitals and then he 'bummed' (buggered) you. After the older boys 'bummed' the younger ones they went out to play. You had to do it if you wanted to play with Smith and his gang. It hadn't happened twice, but most of the time when he was home since he was four years old. They had been a gang. This was what they did before going out to play.

Colin's fear of seeing Smith in court was not because he was scared of Smith for sexually abusing him, but because he had betrayed Smith, the gang leader. That was his gang and the ritual had been going on for five years in various forms. When the abuse had been discovered, he had betrayed the Leader and the gang had split up.

Colin's disclosure of the gang ritual was a crucial moment in our work together. The ritual mirrored much of what Colin had seen and feared in his mother's relationships with men. Relationships were about power, power of the violent over the physically weak and sex was one way of exerting or submitting to this power.

One difficulty for Colin was that, in order to accommodate the physical and sexual violence, he had desensitized himself. After the disclosure, Colin felt safe enough to explore appropriate sensations and we developed many pleasurable awareness activities. We began embodiment play. His favourite sensation was to blow bubbles out of the playroom window. Small, tiny compensations for the loss of childhood where play with other children had been so distorted by sex and violence.

At the same time, I tried to help Colin develop some personal autonomy, so that he could control his behaviour and not feel the need to submit to the sexual or violent demands of other adults or children. While Colin responded with the appropriate verbal responses, it was not clear if he was just being accommodating to adult demands on him. He explained the power of the ritual which had gone on for so long that it had made the bonds of the gang strong. We made masks of the gang leader and gang members and enacted the ritual to see if Colin could develop some resistance. He had said he would say 'no' now to the gang, but as we began to re-enact his gang, he showed he had no power to resist. He was shocked by the power that the rituals still held for him. We decided we needed to make new rituals and stories to take away the power of the gang. We started a new and productive phase of play. Through developing stories, Colin was able to acknowledge his feelings of anger about his mother's and his own powerlessness and victimization. Colin evolved a story about a snake and a ghost, which was forever haunting the snake. The task of the snake was to grow arms, legs and turn into a human being, in fact a Prince. The task of the ghost was to haunt the snake, reminding him of his obligations if he is to become human. When the snake becomes human, if ever, then the ghost can return to ghostland; if the snake stays snake then the ghost goes on haunting.

At the beginning Colin wrote, 'The snake is a pain in the bum. I hope he gets better soon.' The ghost, I'm afraid, was just bossy.

The journey was not without serious difficulties. After a short holiday at home Colin wrote the following story:

> The ghost went on holiday and the snake began to misbehave. He wriggled about in the forest interfering with everybody else and annoying them. He bit a girl on her face on her cheek, she screamed, hit the snake, but he went after her and killed her. He lived in a tree for quite a while and lay in the sun. He was good tempered until people came then the snake bit all of them, went after all of them and killed them.
>
> Then the ghost came back. She was cross. The snake fidgeted about and drove her mad.
>
> She told the snake to shut up and sit down or else . . .

It was after this story that Colin acknowledged he had been abusing two young children in the holiday. He felt compelled to tell me, but angry at the same time. He drew a picture, threw it at me and said it was a drawing of a bum with shit coming out. 'I'm the bum and you're the shit.'

We went on working together. Colin was challenged about his abusive behaviour and often got angry. We had to find ways for the snake to become a prince. The ghost went on haunting, very fierce sometimes, making strict rules to keep everybody as safe as possible.

The Snake and the Ghost

> Once upon a time there was a snake. He was generous and if there was trouble in the jungle he would attack like a dog.
>
> One day the snake was slithering in the jungle when he met a ghost. The ghost was horrible because she shouted. The snake was angry so the snake poisoned him with his tongue and the ghost said 'Stop it, you can't hurt me because I'm a ghost'. The snake's tongue went right through the ghost.

The ghost said 'I shall haunt you for ever unless you find out who you really are because I know that once upon a time you were a prince and a bad magician changed you into a snake so everybody would be frightened of you. If you find the magic wand of the magician you will be changed into a prince and I can go back to ghostland—but if you don't I shall haunt you for ever'.

The snake climbed up the mountain then he saw an island with snakes so he went up to them and he said 'Have you seen the magician?'. They said 'South'.

The snake went South, saw a castle. He went to the castle and saw the magician. He was old and had a long beard flowing from his cheeks. The snake asked if he had a wand. The magician said yes and gave him the wand.

The snake went back to the jungle but couldn't find the ghost but the next day the ghost knocked on his door and said 'Have you got the wand?'. The snake said yes and gave her the wand, then the ghost turned him back into a prince. So the ghost went back to ghostland and the prince married a princess. They had two children and they were kind to the children and to each other and they didn't fight.

Colin was eventually fostered and he has had difficulties and troubles in his search to be likeable to himself and caring in his relationships with others.

We have parted. The snake has left the ghost except in memory. The snake is not quite a Prince. The struggle to resist being the monster goes on for Colin.

Alex's Stories

Alex's father was in all senses a monster. Alex lived in terror of him, even though he had not seen him for five years. He didn't feel safe; can he ever feel safe? How can we get rid of the monster? How can we come to terms with such terror?

Alex had been abused by his father some years ago, in another country. He was now twelve and had lived with his fears for some years. He told me his stories to get rid of the fear, to try to stop the nightmares, to help him go on with his life.

The Monster

There was once a man who was a monster. He was terrifying. The worst thing he did was kill people with a knife. Other people saw this monster kill people with a knife and they were afraid. He was jealous of everybody, he had no friends, he done bad things.

So monster, I hate you. You're mean, crazy, mad. How are such monsters made? We are safe from this monster until dreaming of him and then we have to change into Indiana Jones and bullwhip him out of our dreams.

The monster says, 'I am going to sex you and kill you'. But Indiana Jones says, 'I have power to stop you.'

Then the monster says 'No you can't.' But Indiana Jones says, 'See if I can't' and takes out his magic whip and whips the power from the monster. And the monster turns into a snake and is trapped by Indiana Jones in a cage. The monster tries changing into a stronger animal but the whip is magic and he is trapped, alive and squirming and fairly safe unless he can break out. We hope not.

Alex imagined he was Indiana Jones in his nightmares and they became less frequent. We played about escaping from the monster if he came and we devised lots of strategies to cope with this. Alex started to smile and not hide his face away.

The next story was still about the monster but also perhaps about the sense of being displaced, living in a strange country, never able to return to the place to which you belong because of the monster.

Tim's Story

There was once a boy called Tim and he came from the Moon. You can play, jump about, go places from the Moon to the Stars and back again. You can go to other planets. One day Tim went on a journey. He got into a rocket and went to earth. The rocket was comfortable and he went to sleep on the way.

When he woke up he was stuck. He got out of the rocket and fell into the quicksand. There was a house nearby, some people lived there. Tim wants to get there to know where he is but he can't.

Tim would like to go back to the Moon, he would travel to other planets. The moon is safe.

The monster is stopping Tim. The monster is a ghost. When you try going anywhere he comes in front of you. He has mean eyes, a mouth and long arms. He walks like a jelly. He stands in front of you.

Tim tries to run but can't get away. The arms of the monster reach out. Perhaps the only way to get rid of the monster is to become one.

When Alex wrote this story he had just about decided that life might be worth living. He was then able to express his fear that to get rid of the monster you have to become the monster.

My response was firm. There must be other ways. Alex was surprised by my vehemence and made a decision to explore further.

He wrote his final story about the monster.

The Monster and How to get Rid of Him

The monster is called Harry. He is red and he is a ghost. He has mean eyes, green hair and a mouth with teeth like sharp swords. If you get your fingers in the way of the teeth they fall off.

His arms are long and strong. He scares people with his arms and his fingers. He touches hair, all the holes in the body, on the face and everywhere even the most private parts. He touches to hurt. He chases with his feet. He holds people with his hands, he doesn't care about the other person he just goes on. He wants people to like what he does but if they don't like it he doesn't stop.

He is an old ghost and chases boys and girls not people like himself.

This monster hates to see his own reflection. He doesn't like people to stand up to him. If you do he runs away.

After making his stories Alex spent many sessions playing and drawing without saying anything. He drew monsters, attacked the monster dolls and spent many sessions in tactile play. As he became aware of his senses, he began to make eye contact then he talked, he smiled. He felt he could come and just play if he wanted to with no expectations on my part.

Alex recently told me he didn't want to talk about the monster now. He wanted to play about himself. This monster is hard to leave behind, to lose, without being sucked into its way of being. This is the conflict that Alex wants to resolve. It isn't easy to go on living and not become the monster, to go on living and not become the victim. Alex is learning to free himself a little from his past.

How hard the road to be a survivor.

Getting Rid of the Monster. Ways of Coping

When children who have been sexually abused come to Play Therapy they have very mixed feelings about the way they coped with their abuse. It is not easy for a child to stop abuse if the perpetrator is a family member, friend of the family or physically stronger and bigger than they are. During the course of play we often look at ways of dealing with monsters, accepting that whatever strategy works is appropriate.

von Franz states that there are stories which say that if you meet evil you must fight it, but there are just as many which say that you must run away and not try to fight it. Some say to suffer without hitting back, other's say don't be a fool, hit back!

> There are stories which say that if you are confronted with evil the only thing to do is to lie your way out of it; others say no, be honest, even towards the devil, don't be involved with lying (von Franz 1974).

Whatever the stories say, at the end of the day we try to do what we can in the circumstances. Von Franz (1974) states that we can say that in human nature it would be right to do this or that but in the end I am going to do this the third thing which is my choice as an individual

When I play with children who have experienced abuse, I sometimes tell them stories which describe ways of dealing with monsters. Sometimes it is a comfort to a child to connect with a hero who dealt with the monster in the same way as they did. For other children it offers strategies and ways to cope. And for all, it's a story with it's own resonance.

Here are three strategies. The first story is about tricking the monster:

Escaping Slowly

A goat was walking along with her two kids looking for some nice sweet grass when it began to rain. It was really coming down, so she ran under a big rock ledge to get some shelter, not knowing that it was Lion's house. When Lion saw the three goats coming, he purred to himself in a voice like thunder.

This frightened the mother and her kids and she said, 'Good evening, Minister.' And the lion said, 'Good evening.' She said she was looking for a minister to baptize these two kids, because she wanted to give them names. Lion said he'd be happy to do that: 'This one's name is Dinner and this one's name is Breakfast Tomorrow and your name is Dinner Tomorrow.'

So now after hearing this roared out by Lion, the goats were really frightened, and the kids' hearts began to leap. Lion asked the mother goat what was the matter with her two kids and she said, 'Well, they are always feeling this way when the room they are in gets so hot.' So she asked Lion that since they were feeling that way, could they go out and get a little cool air.

Lion agreed that they could go out until dinner time, but they must come back in. So the mother whispered to the two kids to run as hard as they could until dark came.

So when the lion saw that evening was falling, and he didn't see the kids coming back, he started to roar again. Mother goat said that she was wondering why they were staying out so long, so she asked Lion if she shouldn't go out and get them before it got too dark. The lion agreed. And as soon as the mother got out, she really took off running.

Children enjoy the cleverness of the goat in this story and laugh at the stupidity of the Lion, so strong yet so silly. This next story from Central and South Africa has many resonances for small girls. It is a story about endurance, holding on to any nurture you can and still hanging on when more and more is taken from you. This is the experience of many young children who are abused in the family.

The Girl and the Tree

Once upon a time there was a young girl who lived with her father and stepmother and this woman was very cruel to her. Every so often the girl sat crying by her mother's grave and one day as she sat crying she saw the earth part and a green shoot pushing its way out. The shoot grew into a strong sapling and then into a strong tree. The wind rustled the leaves of the tree and the tree whispered to the girl to pick and eat the fruit. The girl ate the fruit of the tree and began to feel better.

Every day the girl went to the tree for more fruit.

She became so happy her stepmother began to notice and one day followed her to the tree. She saw the girl eat the fruit. That evening the wicked step-mother told her husband to cut down the tree. At first he refused but his wife nagged and nagged until in the end he had the tree chopped down.

The girl wept on the trunk of the broken tree. As she wept she saw a small round lump growing from the lifeless trunk of the tree. It grew into a firm, round pumpkin from which juice began to trickle out. The girl drank the juice and felt better.

Her stepmother saw this and again followed the girl.

She dug up the pumpkin and threw it on the dung heap. The girl went back and found a tiny stream trickling from the trunk of the tree. But her stepmother found out and had the stream buried under a heap of sand.

The next day the girl sat crying on her mother's grave and a young man came by. He saw the dead tree and thought it would make a fine bow and strong arrows.

The girl told him that the tree once grew on her mother's grave. The two began to talk and they took a liking to each other and decided to marry.

They went home to tell her father who agreed on condition that the young man shoot twelve buffaloes for the marriage feast. The young man was worried. He had never shot more than one buffalo at a time.

However, taking his new bow and arrow he set off and it was not long before he saw a herd of twelve buffaloes. He set his arrow in the bow and took aim. Much to his surprise, the first buffalo fell dead and he quickly shot the other animals.

The young man went back to the village to tell the father who sent men to collect the buffalo. There was a great feast and the hunter married the girl and they lived happily ever after. The mother's spirit could rest in peace at last.

For many children. the hunter who makes a bow and arrows from the nurturing tree represents finding strength within yourself through nurturing yourself to become strong enough to separate from the cruelty of the monster.

This last story from St. Vincent tells of direct confrontation with the monster and for some it represents what we might experience on the therapeutic journey. In play, feeling safe, we might confront our monsters, but even if we are strong enough, we need a little magic to help and we have to crawl inside the monster, not once but many times before it is left behind. A messy business!

And in an ideal world how nice to have a granny, a loving wife, a house and a car as a reward.

Loggerhead

Once upon a time there was a big bird called Loggerhead in the village and everybody had to pass this bird on their way home from work.

This bird flew out of his tree every day and picked up one person walking home and swallowed them whole.

Old Witch Boy lived with his grandmother and he began thinking about this bird and how he could stop him eating all the villagers. He wanted to know how a bird could get so strong as to swallow a person whole. He thought about all kinds of magic until one day he saw a special piece of tin on a roof. He told his granny he was going to get that tin and make a special knife. So he got the tin and he made a knife with a handle and sharpened the knife. When his grandmother saw him she began to cry. She said 'Grandson, you're the only family I have left on earth. If you go after that bird you'll lose your life'. He said 'Don't be frightened for me. I'll go and cool everything for everybody'. And he went off up the road with his little knife.

When he reached the tree he began to sing a little song

Coo-Cayima, Coo-Cayima

Loggerhead, Loggerhead

Right away this big bird came down and picked the boy up still singing his little song and he swallowed him whole. And Old Witch Boy took out his little knife and started to cut a hole in the bird's belly, right in the belly until he had cut a hole through and dropped to the ground. Then he walked about under the tree singing his song in a kind of boastful way and the bird flew down again and picked him up. This bird was a big bird, you know, a marvel on that small island. Now when Old Witch Boy had been swallowed up many times and made about three holes in Loggerhead's belly the bird was dead and the boy had made the world clean for others.

Massa King had made a promise that any man that killed the bird would get his daughter, a house and even a new car. So the Witch Boy married immediately.

And there the story ends. Right there.

CHAPTER 8

The Therapist's Journey

It is a hard journey for the therapist to make to accompany children from abuse to healing. There is no 'happy ever after'; wounds may perhaps heal, but scars remain. How to make sense of the inhumanity of abuse to little children? How to stay human amidst such inhumanity? Sometimes the stories of abuse send the therapist reeling, shocked and disgusted by their cruelty. Sometimes the therapist is abused by child or family; sometimes she herself becomes abusive, sucked into the child's need for negative relationships.

The therapist loses her innocence; simple physical contact loses its simplicity, and memories of children's stories of abuse contaminate sexual relationships. Anxiety about the vulnerability of our own children and grandchildren creates fear. At the worst of times, the therapist feels frail, powerless in the face of corruption; when times are better, she is strong in her capacity to help.

Helping can also become 'addictive' to the exclusion of everything else. The therapist becomes damaged and such 'addiction' can induce total burn out. In this state of 'addiction' perspectives become confused and the therapist is unable to tolerate the pain and suffering of her clients' so tries to alleviate it all. She becomes afraid of making mistakes and thinks that taking care of herself is somehow bad for the children.

The therapist needs to understand the emotional effects of her work on herself and also recognise the wider factors of workplace organisation which can also reinforce the helplessness of the therapist. The difficulties of the work must be acknowledged and validated by managers and workers in the agencies who use therapists.

To keep the children safe the therapist must also stay safe. She must seek help and supervision, share and burden, know when to stop and rest. Have time away from the work, other things to do and enjoy. Find a safe place to stay contained; a place to travel towards in the imagination and in reality.

For me, in imagination, I seek a timeless place. I sit on the banks of the Nile at Luxor, the ancient city of Thebes. I look across the river Nile towards the Valley of the Kings, that great burial place. I watch the sun set over the valley as I sit in the city of the living, and between the two, the Valley of the Kings and the City of Thebes, the Nile flows endlessly. Across the river from bank to bank sail the boats. The sun sets, the river flows, and the sun will rise again.

> I sail a long river and row back again. It is joy to breathe under the stars. I am the sojourner destined to walk a thousand years until I arrive at myself (Ellis 1988).

References

Axline, V. (1947/1969) *Play Therapy*. New York: Ballantine Books.

Axline, V. (1955) 'Play therapy procedures and results'. *American Journal of Orthopsychiatry*. 25. 618–626.

Basho, (1966) *The Narrow Road to the Deep North*. Harmondsworth: Penguin.

Bateson, G. (1971) The Message 'This is Play' in R. E. Heron & B. Sutton-Smith (eds) *Child's Play*. New York: Wiley.

Blake, W. 'Infant Sorrow' (1934) *Shakespeare to Hardy*. London: Methuen.

Bolton, F., Morris, L., MacEachron, A. (1989) *Males at Risk: The Other Side of Sexual Abuse*. London: Sage Publications.

Bolton, G. (1979) *Towards a Theory of Drama in Education*. London: Longman.

Borges, J. L. (1974) *The Book of Imaginary Beings*. London: Penguin.

Bretherton, I. (1984) *Symbolic Play*. New York: Academic Press.

Bruner, J. (1972) 'Nature and Uses of Immaturity' in Bruner, J. (ed.) *Play: Its Role in Development and Evolution*. Harmondsworth: Penguin.

Butler-Sloss, Lord Justice. (1988) *Report of the Inquiry into Child Abuse in Cleveland 1987*. London: HMSO.

Caldwell Cook. (1917) *The Play Way*. London: Heinemann.

Courtney, R. (1985) 'The dramatic metaphor and learning' in Kase-Polisini, J. (ed) *Creative Drama in a Developmental Context*. London: University Press of America.

Cutler, I. (1984) *Large et Puffy*. Todmorden: Arc Publications.

Donaldson, M. A. & Gardner, R. (1985) 'Diagnosis and treatment of traumatic stress among women after childhood incest' in C. R. Figley (ed) *Trauma and Its Wake*. New York: Bruner/Mazel.

Ellis, N. (transl) (1988) *Awakening Osiris: The Egyptian Book of the Dead*. Grand Rapids: Phanes Press.

Franz, M. L. von (1987) *Shadow and Evil in Fairytales*. Dallas: Spring Publ.

Frederick, C. J. (1985) 'Children traumatised by catastrophic situations' in S. Eth & R. S. Pynoos (eds) *Post-traumatic Stress Disorder in Children*. Washington DC: American Psychiatric Press.

Freeman, M. (1987) 'Taking Children's Rights Seriously'. *Children & Society*. Vol 1. No 4. 299–319.

Freud, A. (1936) *The Ego and the Mechanisms of Defence*. London: Hogarth.

Freud, A. (1928) 'Introduction to the Techniques of Child Analysis'. *Nerv. Ment. Dis Monograph* No 48.

Freud, S. (1922) *Beyond the Pleasure Principle*. London: Hogarth.

Garvey, C. & Berndt, R. (1977) 'Organisation of Pretend Play'. *JSAS Catalog of Selected Documents in Psychology* 7. (Ms. No. 1589).

Garvey, C. (1977/1990) *Play*. Cambridge, Mass: Harvard University Press.

Gersie, A. (1987) 'Dramatherapy and Play' in Jennings, S. (ed) *Dramatherapy Theory and Practice for Teachers and Clinicians*. Kent: Croom Helm.

Grainger, R. (1990) *Drama and Healing: The Roots of Drama Therapy*. London: Jessica Kingsley Publishers.

Grant, J. (1991) *The State of the World's Children*. Oxford: OUP.

Groos, H. (1901) *The Play of Man*. London: Heinemann.

Haddawy, A. H. (1990) *The Arabian Nights*. New York: Norton.

Heathcote, D. (1980) 'From the particular to the universal' in Robinson, K. (ed) *Exploring Theatre and Education*. London: Heinemann.

Huizinga, J. (1955) *Homo Ludens*. Boston: Beacon Press.

Isaacs, S. (1933) *Social Development in Young Children*. London: Routledge.

Jansson, T. (1987) *Tales From Moomin Valley*. London: Penguin Books.

Jennings, S. (1990) *Dramatherapy with Families, Groups and Individuals, Waiting in the Wings*. London: Jessica Kingsley Publishers.

Jung, C. G. (1931) *The Aims of Psychotherapy*. Collected Works. Vol. 16.

Kempe, R. S. & C. H. (1978) *Child Abuse*. Shepton Mallet: Fontana/Open Books.

Klein, M. (1932) *The Psychoanalysis of Children*. London: Hogarth.

Martin, H. & Beezley, P. (1977) 'Behavioral Observations of Abused Children'. *Developmental Medicine and Child Neurology*. Vol. 19. 373–387

Miller, A. (1988) *The Drama of Being a Child*. London: Virago Press.

Miller, A. (1990) *Banished Knowledge*. London: Virago Press.

Miller, A. (1983) *For Your Own Good*. London: Virago Press.

Moustakas, C. (1953/1974) *Children in Play Therapy*. New York: Ballantine Books.

National Children's Bureau. (1990) *A Policy for Young Children*. London:

Pringle, M. Kellmer (1974) *The Needs of Children*. London: Hutchinson.

Rank, O. (1932) *Art and Artist*. New York: Agathon Press.

Rutter, M. (1991) *Maternal Deprivation Reassessed*. London: Penguin.

Schechter, M. & Roberge, L. (1976) 'Child Sexual Abuse' in Helter, R. and Kempe, C. (eds) *Child Abuse and Neglect: The Family and the Community*, Cambridge, Mass: Ballinger.

Schiller, F. (1875) *Essays Aesthetical and Philosophical*. Bell.

SCOSAC. (1984) 'Definition of Child Sexual Abuse'. Standing Conference on Sexually Abused Children, London.

Sendak, M. (1970) *Where The Wild Things Are*. Harmondsworth: Penguin Books.

Slade, P. (1954) *Child Drama*. London: University of London Press.

Spencer, H. (1873) *Principles of Psychology*. New York: Appleton.

Tagore, R. (1913) *The Crescent Moon*. London: Macmillan.

Terr, L. C. (1981) 'Psychic Trauma in Children'. *American Journal in Psychiatry*, 138, 14–19.

Vygotsky, L. S. (1933) 'Play and its role in the mental development of the child' in Bruner, J. (ed) et al. (1972) *Play: Its Role in Development and Evolution*. Harmondsworth: Penguin.

Way, B. (1967) *Development Through Drama*. London: Longman.

Winnicott, D. W. (1971) *Playing and Reality*. London: Tavistock.

Winterson, J. (1989) *Sexing the Cherry*. London: Bloomsbury.

Books For Young Children

Books about making friends

Harper, A. & Hellard, S. (1990) *What Feels Best?* London: Puffin Books

This book is about a small kangaroo who learns to share. Well illustrated, children recognise some of the situations described and it doesn't labour the point. A great favourite with children up to seven and eight.

McPhail, D. (1988) *Something Special.* London: Puffin Books.

This is a story about a badger family and Sam the young badger who is no good at anything until he discovers a talent for painting.

Paola, T. de (1981) *Oliver Button is a Sissy.* London: Methuen.

This is a book about a boy who didn't like to do the things boys are supposed to do. He was teased by children at school and called a sissy. He went to dancing school and took part in a talent competition. He performed his tap dance well but didn't win the competition. He was scared to go back to school because the other children had been at the contest. When he got to school they had crossed out sissy on the school wall and written 'Oliver Button is a star' instead. This book is very popular with boys who are worried about gender issues. I read it every week at the end of the session to one boy who can now repeat it word for word. The final sentence of 'Oliver Button is a star' being shouted in triumph.

Good for seven, eight year olds.

Books about babyhood

Anholt, C. (1988) *When I was a Baby.* London: Heinemann.

Describes a mother answering her young daughter's questions about being a baby, especially about being nurtured. A warm, peaceful, loving book. Children who didn't receive this kind of nurture really enjoy it and they imagine what it might have been like to be a loved child. Very popular with all abused children. It becomes a kind of mourning for a lost babyhood.

Ross, T. (1987) *I Want My Potty*. London: Collins Publishing.

About a princess learning to use her potty. Very funny and enjoyed by children involved in embodiment play or regressive play. Older children get a giggle from it. Very popular.

Miller, V. (1991) *On Your Potty*. London: Walker Books.

Another funny book about a bear trying to use his potty. 'There are days when Bartholomew is naughty and other days when he is very very good.' The only word he says is 'nah' to whatever he is asked. Very funny illustrations and the adult nurturing bear is George.

Konigslow, A. W. von (1985) *Toilet Tales*. Toronto: Annick Press Ltd.

Describes why toilets are for children and why animals can't use them. Funny illustrations. Loved and laughed at by young children and those who like to drink toilet water!

Cole, B. (1987) *The Smelly Book*. London: Jonathan Cape.

Cole, B. (1985) *The Slimy Book*. London: Jonathan Cape.

Both these books are fun for children involved in messy play; lots of really bad smells and slime including slimy food. Very funny and quite disgusting. Greatly enjoyed by children of all ages including me!

Ahlberg, J. & A. (1989) *Bye Bye Baby*. London: Heinemann.

A wonderful book about a baby who has no mummy and has to do everything for himself. The book describes his search for a mummy and then a daddy. He gathers a collection of toys etc. on his search. They join him on his journey but they all say they can't be his mummy.

This book exerts a powerful hold over children who have lost their family, especially those children to be placed for adoption. Pictures of the baby caring for himself and his loneliness, which is so poignant, moves children as they identify with his isolation.

I have read it again and again to children and hear their sigh of contentment when the baby finds a loving home.

Books about children's behaviour and feelings

Oram, H. & Kitamura, S. (1984) *Angry Arthur*. London: Puffin.

This book describes Arthur's temper tantrum when he is so angry that he destroys the house, town, the world and the universe. As he floats on a piece of Mars sitting on his bed he can't even remember what he was angry about. A marvellous sense of infantile power. Loved by all children who feel afraid of their own anger.

Preston E. M. (1976) *The Temper Tantrum Book.* London: Puffin Books.

This shows different animals and their anger with some of the control exerted over them by adults. The lion hates having his hair combed, the tiger his face washed. The only satisfied person is Hippopotamus, who is allowed to play in the mud.

A good book to stimulate children to talk about the way they were nurtured and the little cruelties exerted by those adults who controlled them.

Giff, P. R. (1980) *Today Was A Terrible Day* London: Puffin Books.

Describes Ronald's terrible day at school when everything goes wrong, but it ends with the teacher giving him a sympathetic note about his day which he can actually read. Very popular with six to eight year olds who find school difficult. It highlights those bungled social relationships which are the curse of abused children.

Oran, H. & Kitamura, S. (1987) *In The Attic.* London: Arrow Books Ltd.

A peaceful book about Arthur of 'Angry Arthur' creating an imaginary world and an imaginary friend.

Enjoyed by abused children who use this strategy to cope with their abuse. They enjoy the story and make connections with their own imaginary worlds.

Hutchins, P. (1972) *Titch.* London: Puffin Books.

This is about Titch, the smallest child in the family. Her big brother and sister seem to have all the best toys and objects, however, when they grow a plant Titch has the seed which grows into an enormous plant.

Useful with children trying to find a place for themselves in a family, or for neglected children who are small and frail.

Carlson, N. (1990) *I Like Me.* London: Puffin Books.

Fun drawings about a girl pig who likes herself. Describes taking care of yourself and liking yourself no matter what. A cheerful optimistic book to encourage children's self esteem.

Books about fear of the dark and night time

Stevenson, J. (1987) *What's Under My Bed.* London: Piccolo Picture Books.

Grandpa telling his two grandchildren, Mary Ann and Louie, about being scared of 'things' under his bed and at night when he was a child. Describes lots of children's fears of the dark.

Helps children connect with their own fears.

Denton, K. M. (1988) *Granny Is A Darling.* London: Walker Books Ltd.

Granny comes to visit and shares Billy's bedroom. He is scared when he hears her snoring and thinks there are monsters about, but he sends them away to protect his granny.

Good for those night fears about shapes in the room that turn into monsters.

Waddell, M. & Firth, B. (1989) *The Park in the Dark.* London: Walker Books Ltd.

Three toys go to the park at night to play on the swings but are scared of the dark and run all the way back home. Pictures of all those objects that change at night, trees with faces, plants coming alive. The three toys are very cuddly.

Wright, C. (1991) *When The World Sleeps.* London: Random Century Children's Books.

The young boy sees the moon fall from the sky and he bravely goes out into the night to put it back. He takes his dog as companion. No words, just powerful pictures.

Wonderful pictures which show a child solving a problem and overcoming fear. Some pictures quite scary, but children love this book.

Books about monsters

Impey, R. (1988) *The Flat Man.* Andover: Ragged Bear Ltd.

Quite scary, about a boy who imagines a flat man who creeps into his bedroom at night. The flat man is scared of light and the boy gets rid of him by flashing a torch in his face.

The description of the flat man as all embracing, wrapping himself around the boy's chest is powerful imagery for the sexually abused child who might find this book too frightening. However, some children are comforted by a book which so powerfully represents their experience. There are other monster books in this series of 'Creepies'.

Ross, T. (1984) *I'm Coming To Get You.* London: Puffin Books.

Beautifully illustrated book about a monster from outer space who comes to earth to 'get' Tommy Brown. Finally. the monster pounces and it is revealed that on earth the monster is only the size of a matchstick.

This book is requested again and again by children on the road to recovery from abuse. Shared laughter is very potent in healing hurt.

Martin, R. & Siow, J. (198?) *There's a Dinosaur In The Park.* Flinders Park, South Australia: Era Publications.

Charming pictures of a boy confronting a dinosaur in the park which might just be a rubbish bin. Not scary and suitable for very young children.

Sendak, M. (1970) *Where The Wild Things Are*. London: Puffin Books.
The classic tale of Max the naughty child and his journey to the land of the monsters and back again to his own bedroom. Has a timeless quality which is soothing to children.

McPhail, D. (1983) *Alligators Are Awful*. London: Octopus Publishing.
Describes the rude, ill-mannered activities of alligators which might possibly be the way some adults and some children behave.
Children sometimes connect this story with their own carer who is as rude, needy and demanding as the alligator; and it's a good giggle.

McKee, D.(1987) *Not Now Bernard*. London: Arrow Books.
My personal favourite, the story of Bernard whose parents are so busy with other tasks they fail to notice that he has turned into a monster. Poor Bernard, even as a monster, gets no attention.
Special for all abused children. Very sad with the constant refrain 'Not now Bernard.'

Books about death

Burningham, J. (1984) *Grandpa*. London: Puffin Books.
Describes the relationship between grandpa and granddaughter and the feeling of emptiness his death brings. Love and the sadness of loss experienced through the pictures. A very gentle book.

Wilhelm, H. (1985) *I'll Always Love You*. London: Hodder & Stoughton.
The story of a boy and the death of his elderly dog. The comfort for the child is that he always told Elfie the dog that he loved her.
This book is loved by children and adults and many tears are shed when reading it. Helpful for children living with someone who is dying because it shows ways to give love and the consolation that this brings when death finally happens.

Varley, S. (1984) *Badger's Parting Gifts*. London: Collins Publishing Group.
Describes the death of Badger and the grieving experienced by his friends. Strong imagery for the process of death—going down 'the long tunnel' and the way we cope with loss through memory.
Helps children say goodbye and begin to let go.

A Book for comfort

Mazer, A. (1990) *The Yellow Button*. London: Head Children's Books.
Beautiful pictures describing a yellow button in a dress pocket having its own place in the universe. Very soothing.

Books about keeping safe

My two particular favourites about body boundaries and nurturing needs do not particularly emphasise keeping safe from sexual abuse, but make general comments about ownership of your own body.

We do force children into physical contact with adults which they do not want, often for politeness sake, yet expect the same children to discriminate abusing adults. The advert of a child scrubbing granny's lipstick off his lips after an unwanted kiss strikes a chord, and I speak as a granny who does not expect kisses from grandchildren who do not see me often.

Freeman, L. (1986) *Loving Touches*. Seattle: Parenting Press Inc.

This book describes nurturing needs; food, warmth and 'loving touches to make me feel just right'. It describes different kinds of loving touches between children and adults.

This book is much enjoyed by young children up to about seven, for both learning and, perhaps, imagining the kind of parenting which was not received by unnurtured children.

Freeman, L. (1982) *It's My Body*. Seattle: Parenting Press Inc.

This book firmly establishes that the child's body belongs to the child and describes a variety of ways to share your body and discusses times when you don't want to share your body. This book is very popular with young children, as the messages are simple and direct and create a sense of pride about the body and ownership of the body.

Hart-Rossi, (1984) *Protect Your Child From Sexual Abuse. A Parent's Guide*. Seattle: Parenting Press Inc.

This book accompanies 'It's My Body', explaining ways of using the book and providing activities for young children to help keep them safe.

Davis, D. (1984) *Something Is Wrong At My House*. Seattle Parenting Press Inc.

This book describes what it is like living in a violent household where parents fight, discussing how the child feels and what he or she can do about it.

This is a very valuable book for both young and older children and has proved comforting and helpful.

Kehoe, P. (1987) *Something Happened and I'm Scared To Tell*. Seattle: Parenting Press Inc.

This book is about a conversation between a child and an imaginary lion in which the child tells about sexual abuse and the lion gives advice. Very helpful explanations about abuse and not keeping secrets. Good messages to the child.

Peake, A. & Khadj, R. (1989) *My Book My Body*. London: The Children's Society.

Good colouring book about body boundaries for young children.

Hessell, J. (1987) *What's Wrong With Bottoms?* London: Hutchinsons Children's Books.

This book describes Uncle Henry exposing himself to his nephew and how it was dealt with in the family. Very useful for all boys abused by men. Seeing the problem illustrated in a book helps to understand that they are not the only ones. The book gives information about the importance of telling someone.

Saphira, M. & McIntyre, L. (1989) *Look Back Stride Forward.* Aukland, New Zealand: Papers Inc.

An excellent book for older children and adolescents about how abuse affects the lives of children. Clear descriptions of difficulties experienced by abused children and suggestions for healing.

Very popular book. Helps children gain confidence and understanding.

Sex education

I have found that the books by Peter Mayle and Arthur Robins give clear information about sex and that the cartoon format is very helpful to abused children, especially sexually abused children, who find the books non-threatening.

Mayle, P. & Robins, A. (1978) *Where Did I Come From?* London: MacMillan Ltd.

Good book for young children about the birth of a baby. The pictures are the best thing about the book and can be used with very young children to explain what sex is for. Sometimes you have to explain to very young children that sperm don't have eyes, nose and mouth and they don't wear top hats as illustrated in the book, but that's all part of the fun.

Mayle, P. & Robins, A. (1975) *What's Happening To Me?* London: MacMillan Ltd.

Good guide to puberty and includes 'the world's most embarrassing questions'.

Mayle, P. & Robins, A. (1981) *We're Not Pregnant. London:* Macmillan Ltd.

Good pre-Aids book about birth control. Funny, rude illustrations which appeal.

Blank, J. & Quackenbush, M. *The Playbook for Kids about Sex.* London: Sheba Feminist Publishers.

Some people find this book offensive, with its vivid descriptions about masturbation, sexual intercourse and different kinds of sexual relationships. It has been banned in places, but I find the descriptions of aspects of sex very clear for young children.

Meredith, S. (1985) *Growing Up*. London: Usborne Publishing Ltd.

No nonsense guide to adolescence and sex, including more general advice on diet and cleanliness.

Saint Phalle, N. de (1987) *Aids: You Can't Catch It Holding Hands*. San Francisco: The Lapis Press.

Good illustrated book about aids, mostly bright illustrations and simple but effective text. Not patronising. Useful for young children and adolescents. Sadly, this book will be more in demand for young children.